SHOWING

SHOWING

Jane Holderness-Roddam

THRESHOLD BOOKS

First published in Great Britain by
Threshold Books Ltd
661 Fulham Road
London SW6 5PZ
1989

British Library Cataloguing in Publication Data

Holderness-Roddam, Jane
Showing.
1. Livestock: Horses. Showing
I. Title
636.1'0888

ISBN 0-901366-55-2

Photographs by Bob Langrish
Line drawings by Dianne Breeze
Designed by Paul Saunders

Typeset by PPC Limited, Leatherhead, Surrey
Printed and bound in Great Britain by Richard Clay Ltd, Bungay, Suffolk

FRONTISPIECE *Elite – an outstanding champion with tremendous presence – being admired by the judges at the Royal Windsor Horse Show, 1986.*

CONTENTS

PREFACE

Showing is the art of presenting your horse at its best so that it catches the eye and impresses the judge, and knowing some of the tips employed by the professionals can make a tremendous difference as to how the judge sees your horse. This book aims to provide some of those tricks of the trade, and will serve as a practical guide and reference for anyone involved in showing horses and ponies both in-hand and ridden.

The first section of the book covers the general aspects of horse care, training, turn-out and ringcraft involved in the preparation and presentation of an animal for the show ring. Useful advice on how to make the most of the horse's good points and disguise its less good features is included, as well as guidance on the pitfalls of showing.

The last section provides useful reference charts giving information on all the main types of classes catered for in Britain today. While fashions and trends may change these charts aim to reflect the accepted way of conducting the numerous classes that exist for virtually every type of horse and pony, and provide an indication of what can be expected in those classes, as well as the correct tack and clothes, type of show, whether the judge rides and other relevant information which may be helpful.

Over the years I have been asked many questions about showing and have often had to go and find out for myself how certain things are done; it is to be hoped, therefore, that this book will fill a gap in showing literature and provide a useful handbook for all who wish to show their horses or ponies.

ACKNOWLEDGEMENTS

The author would like to acknowledge with grateful thanks the assistance she received from Lucy Gemmell, Jennie Nelson and Helen Sainsbury who painstakingly typed the manuscript and helped with the research for the book. She would also like to thank Mrs N. de Quincey; Mr and Mrs R. Gifford; Jennie and Anne Loriston-Clarke; Bob Langrish for his superb photographs; Dianne Breeze for her excellent line drawings; and the following societies for their helpful information:

National Pony Society; British Appaloosa Society; Western Horseman's Association of Great Britain; Shire Horse Society; British Trakehner Association; British Percheron Horse Society; British Morgan Horse Society; Thoroughbred Breeders' Association; Clydesdale Horse Society of Great Britain and Ireland; British Quarter Horse Association; American Saddlebred Association of Great Britain and Ireland; British Spotted Pony Society; Arab Horse Society; Icelandic Horse Society of Great Britain; British Andalusian Horse Society; British Caspian Society; Haflinger Society of Great Britain; National Light Horse Breeding Society (HIS); British Warmblood Society; Hackney Horse Society; Cleveland Bay Horse Society; English Connemara Pony Society Ltd; British Lipizzaner Horse Society; British Show Hack, Cob and Riding Horse Association; British Show Pony Society; and Fallabella Society.

PART 1

Showing and Ringcraft

Mrs Robert Oliver on board the champion large hack, Rye Tangle, at Windsor, 1988.

CHAPTER · 1

AN INTRODUCTION TO SHOWING

What is a show horse? This is quite difficult to answer but perhaps the show horse can be best described as the most nearly perfect example of the type or breed of animal it represents.

Conformation

Conformation plays a very big part in the show animal, so perhaps it would be as well to go through each part of the horse and briefly discuss what the judge is looking for. The overall impression, however, is likely to be the deciding factor at the end of the day.

The **head** is probably the most important feature and must be in proportion to the rest of the body and pleasing to the eye. In certain classes it will have to conform to rules for that particular type. The way it is set on to the neck and how it is carried are what will be noticed by the judge, and the whole bearing and presence of the horse does seem to be governed by the head.

The **neck** should be nicely muscled and come out from well-shaped withers. It should be well proportioned with a good top-line and not have an overdeveloped bottom line. The neck should not be set on too low, i.e. coming out the shoulders, and should be nicely curved. The arch of the head and neck is the crucial factor in defining presence, which is so important in the show horse.

The **back** should be strong and well proportioned, which is really more important than whether it is a little too long or very short coupled. It should be well muscled on either side of the back bone, and in the ridden show horse the rider should appear to be sitting in the middle so that the overall picture looks in proportion.

The **quarters** should be strong and rounded, and well muscled on top and between the hind legs. Hind legs that are 'split up the back' indicate weakness, as do quarters which slope away from the backbone. When seen from behind, the horse should be well muscled and give a strong and balanced view on either side.

The **shoulders** should be nicely sloping and have plenty of freedom. A very straight shoulder indicates lack of freedom, resulting in a short or choppy stride and rarely a good ride. The 'stuffy' or 'overloaded' shoulder will usually offer the same restricted movement. Look at the horse from the front to ensure there is some width between the front legs; they should not 'come out of one hole'.

The **body** should be rounded and well proportioned so that shoulders, body and quarters all join up well together. The ribs should be well sprung and rounded, giving the horse 'depth' or a 'good girth'. A shallow horse indicates weakness following the theory that there is insufficient room for the heart and lungs to develop to their full capacity. The saddle should sit well back behind the shoulder with the shape of the body allowing for this.

The **limbs** – 'bone' is the essential element where the limbs are concerned and it is the amount of bone which is the deciding factor in

A lovely stamp of horse with the essential ingredients of quality, presence and good basic conformation. It is a little short of condition and muscle behind, but careful feeding, strapping and schooling would build this up into a more rounded outline, which is favoured for the show animal.

hunter or weight-carrying classes. Bone is measured just below the knee, round the cannon. It should be flat in preference to being rounded. The smaller, finer breeds may be rather light in this respect but it is the overall picture of proportions that should be considered. Shorter, rather than longer, cannon bones denote strength. The knees should be strong and flat with the limbs coming out straight, both above and below. The cannon bones should be short, hard and flat with the tendons well defined and the fetlock joints flat rather than too rounded. Fleshy-looking legs with very rounded 'apple' joints are not favoured. The pasterns should be gently sloping; upright pasterns cause a 'jarring' action, and those which slope too much denote weakness.

The **hocks** should be a pair, strong and straight. They should have a good angle without too much bend, indicating weakness. If they are too straight mobility is restricted. There should be a definite angle between the hip, stifle joint and hock for good movement of the hind limbs.

The **feet** must be well shaped and in good condition. Good shoeing, with the right shoe for the occasion, is very important. Many a horse with doubtful action has been greatly improved by careful corrective shoeing, so don't completely discount an animal who has, for example, a slight 'dish'. Discuss the matter with your farrier who will advise what can be done to improve it. The judge, however, will be looking for perfection so at the end of the day the horse with the least problems and faults is likely to come out on top. A horse with a good 'pair' of feet will always take preference over one with odd feet.

The overall picture should be pleasing to the eye and the animal must have that extra something which makes it stand out from the others. The quality that says 'look at me', known as **presence,** makes the world of difference to the show horse and often it is this which catches the judge's eye long before the proportions and conformation have been assessed.

Colour

In theory, colour should make little difference but there is no doubt that good strong colours catch the eye. Rich bays, browns and chestnuts seem to head most of the line-ups with greys also being a good colour for the show horse. Wishy-washy colours do not stand out, so a horse of indifferent colour will have to be really good in other respects to ensure it is noticed. In some classes colour is essential to the type and is assessed on its quality. For example, palominos are expected to gleam like a 'newly minted gold coin' and only a minimum amount of dark hairs are allowed in the mane and tail.

The show horse must possess a quality that says 'Look at me'. Alastair Hood and the champion hunter Inspector Cluzeot have caught the judge's eye at the 1988 Royal International Horse Show; they went on to win the Winston Churchill cup for the Supreme Champion Show Horse.

There is no doubt that the show horse will stand out in a class if it has good markings as well as a good colour. A central star or stripe, or not too wide a blaze, can accentuate looks. A pair of white socks, or even four white legs, can look magnificent in a show horse whereas they might be less favoured in other fields of competition. Although it doesn't matter too much visually, one white leg, sock or stocking can slightly unbalance the picture especially if it is in front, and likewise a pair of feet of the same colour is preferable.

Movement

The movement of the horse plays a very big part and a really good mover can rise several places, compensating for minor conformation defects. The rhythm and stride as well as straightness are what count so it is extremely important that the animal is allowed to move and show itself off to its best advantage by its rider or handler. In some classes, such as those for Welsh Cobs, it is essential that the handler can run briskly as the cob is expected to move at a very strong trot in front of the judges to show off its naturally inherent movement.

The type of movement should be reflected by the category of horse or pony being shown. While a hunter would be expected to have a good strong trot, be able to show some extension and also to gallop well, the elegance of the hack should be reflected in its paces. In breeding classes the quality of the movement is important and becoming increasingly more so. The current trend is to be more selective with regard to movement which previously had been rather neglected.

Manners

The way of going and manners will be taken very much into account, and in ridden classes they play a very important role. Children's ponies, hacks and riding horses, in particular, are expected to be perfectly behaved at all times, but all horses, whatever their type or breed, must perform well throughout. Any horse or pony considered by the judge to be not under proper control or ill-mannered is likely to be asked to leave the ring.

On windy days in-hand classes can sometimes become a recipe for disaster with strong two- or three-year-old colts taking charge of the proceedings. Discipline is important from an early age and firm handling is essential for youngsters if they are not to become a danger to everyone, including themselves. It is quite unacceptable to show animals which cannot be controlled and the excuse that the wild thing up on its hind legs or charging round on the end of a leading rein 'is only young' is simply not good enough. Any horse or pony out of control is potentially dangerous and should not be brought out in public until it is sufficiently disciplined to be able to behave reasonably.

The individual show

The show is the one chance the rider has of presenting his horse or pony to the judge without the distractions of the rest of the class so it is essential to make the best possible use of the short time available. The judge will expect to see that the animal has a reasonable walk, so a few strides should be shown before moving into trot, which, if possible, should include some extension. A canter, including a change of rein to show both leads (if time permits), plus a gallop if appropriate to the class, followed by a halt and rein back, and/or canter on to a final halt completes the show. The secret, however, is to fit all this into as short a time as possible. Judges are nearly always pushed for time and a short, sharp show will be far more appreciated than a longer one which may result in other competitors down the line not getting the opportunity to show off their animals, which they will not thank you for.

It is quality rather than quantity that is required and no show should take longer than 1½ minutes if it is done professionally.

The ride

The ride by the judge in such classes as hunters, hacks, cobs, riding horses and some ridden breed classes, can again have a considerable influence on your horse's final placing, so good training and manners when under saddle are very important.

The hunter and cob must give a good workmanlike feel with a positive free-moving performance and be able to really stride on at the gallop, pull up and stand still.

The hack must be beautifully trained and an easy, light ride capable of being ridden 'on the little finger'. It must be responsive, collected and well mannered, and particularly suitable as a lady's ride. Hacks are not expected to gallop but must be able to stride on well, pull up easily, rein back and strike off on either leg. The riding horse should be similarly trained but should gallop on and be a lovely, easy, handy ride capable of doing anything and going anywhere.

The various breed classes, whether they be Shetland, Welsh Cob or riding pony types, should all be good free-moving rides, obedient and well mannered. All the mountain and moorland breeds are hardy tough animals but their rides should be light and easy with comfortable strides. They should be able to gallop on and come back to a halt, and whatever their size they should feel well proportioned and balanced.

The size of the judge must be taken into account so that the saddle and stirrup irons are a good fit, as problems here will not help towards promoting your horse or pony's good points as a ride.

Running up in-hand

Running up in-hand offers the judge a good opportunity of studying your horse close-to and seeing how straight it moves. How you present your horse will very much govern the judge's reaction. The horse or pony must therefore be taught to stand up properly, not take long to adopt a good position and obediently step forwards or backwards as required to give the judge the best possible view. It must lead out well and show itself off at the walk and trot, going straight back past the judge, moving freely and actively to give a good outline.

At this point in the class the judge has the chance to decide whether to move you up or down the line, so knowing how to make the most of your horse is essential.

The above headings briefly cover the main points of showing and outline what the judge will be looking for when assessing a class. The following chapters deal with how to make the most of your horse and present it to its best advantage in the ring. However, there are some horses that will never make a show horse for various reasons and so *what is not a show horse* should perhaps be mentioned before going any further.

Faults

A horse with conformational defects is not going to shine in the show ring and while some faults may go unnoticed at smaller shows, they will not be overlooked at shows higher up the ladder.

Curbs, spavins, thoroughpins and obvious ring- or side-bones will

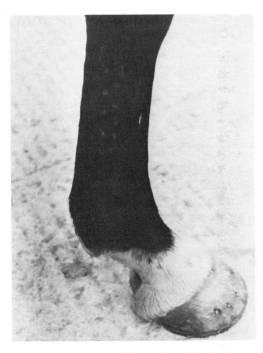

Firing of any sort is generally not tolerated in the show horse and such horses should not be shown.

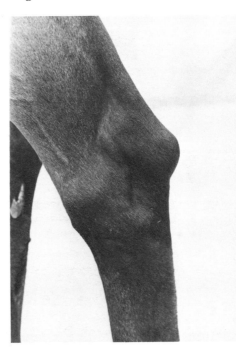

Capped hocks are usually caused by friction, and are often due to lack of bedding. Such blemishes can ruin the prospects of an otherwise perfect show horse so it is worth taking extra care to ensure that such unnecessary problems are avoided.

definitely go right down the line. Splints are tolerated by most judges so long as they are not unsightly and do not interfere with the action of the horse, but the horse without a splint will often be put up if a judge has to choose between two otherwise equal exhibits.

Animals with roached backs, dipped backs, ewe necks, very short necks or very large heads will not make show horses. Those with cow

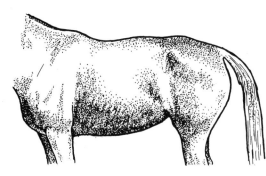

A roached back is difficult to disguise; a horse with such a noticeable fault will never be a success in the show ring.

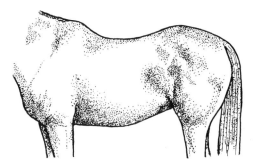

Dipped, hollow or sway backs may be strengthened by giving all feeds on the floor. They are rarely noticeable until the horse is stripped. Keep the horse's head low when in front of the judge!

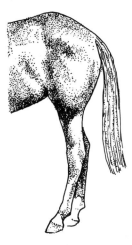

The goose-rumped horse usually has a low-set-on tail. It is not generally favoured but may indicate a good jumper.

Ewe or weak necks can be improved with careful strapping, feeding and schooling. Clever plaiting on top of the neck will help to disguise this problem.

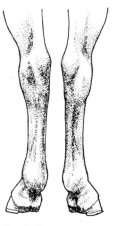

Cow hocks are a conformation defect. The farrier may be able to improve mild cases with corrective shoeing. Don't stand the horse up square behind in front of the judge.

hocks, sickle hocks, club foot, contracted heels, crooked legs and any obvious signs of unevenness such as a dropped hip and a badly crooked spine, will also never make it in the show ring.

Horses that have been operated on for wind or that have been fired or pin fired are barred from all classes judged under official society rules, but they may compete in unaffiliated shows and it is left to the judge's discretion as to whether or not to penalise them; inevitably if there are two horses of similar standing the horse without a problem should beat the other.

A horse which moves badly will also be at a distinct disadvantage especially if it 'dishes' noticeably, turns a foot in, swings a leg, goes very close or 'plaits', and if shoeing cannot help this then your horse will usually be placed lower down the order after being run up in-hand. There have been many handsome horses that would have been champions had they moved better, and there have been champions whose magnificent movement has helped judges to excuse their other faults. So if your horse is a good mover with reasonable conformation it may have a chance in the show ring, but then presentation becomes even more important.

CHAPTER · 2

HEALTH AND CONDITION

The general health and condition of the show animal are vital to success and play a major role towards the final outcome. This book does not intend to go into the finer points of stable management and feeding; rather, it concentrates on the important factors that relate to showing.

Routine health care

The general health of the show horse must be the number one priority so a thorough **worming** routine must be established, with a six- to eight-week cycle being recommended by the veterinary profession. No animal will thrive if it is carrying a worm burden and it is a wise precaution to give any new acquisition a thorough worming to ensure you are giving it the best start, and to discuss the matter with your vet, who may recommend that the horse be tubed. Thereafter you should stick rigidly to your vet's recommended routine.

Equine vaccinations are now generally becoming a necessity whether we like it or not and many showgrounds insist on seeing your horse's certificate. Make sure yours is up to date and corresponds with the requirements. Many horses and ponies have qualified for the Horse of the Year Show and Royal International Horse Show only to be turned away because their flu vaccination certificates were invalid. The annual vaccination should be carried out at a time when your horse is resting rather than working hard.

Tetanus protection is normally included in the vaccination and is a wise precaution. Once the initial dosage is given, boosters are only required biennially.

Teeth care is another important consideration, both to ensure the horse can masticate properly and obtain maximum benefit from its food, and to help keep it comfortable in its mouth so that it goes well without any sharp teeth causing discomfort and encouraging head tossing and general aggravation. It is sensible to have the horse's teeth examined by a vet twice a year and rasped if necessary.

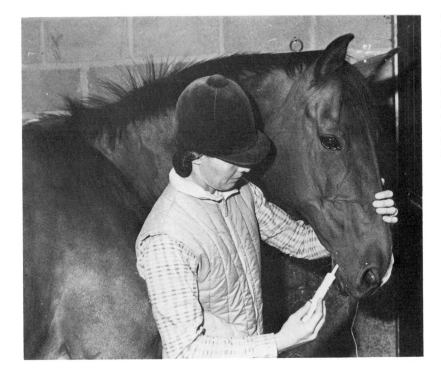

Worming doses should be administered at least every eight weeks. If this is not carried out regularly no amount of feeding and supplements will compensate for the detrimental effects of an internal worm problem.

Feeding

Having ensured your horse's basic health care programme is established, sensible feeding is the next priority. The show horse is required to look well rounded and a picture of health throughout the showing season. The trend of having all show horses grossly fat is very slowly changing. Overfat animals cannot move properly, and in the past many youngsters were ruined by being overfed too young, resulting in all sorts of growth problems. Many became coarse and never achieved their real potential after being overloaded as one-, two- and three-year-olds, and those that were allowed to mature at a more natural rate ended up as the real champions.

Feeding the show horse is a great art. Travelling will take its inevitable toll, particularly if you do a lot of showing, yet you have to keep the condition on without letting the animal get out of hand or overfresh. There is no doubt that a spell in the field every day, in a safe well-fenced paddock, will help tremendously to relax the horse and give him some green food and, it is hoped, some sunlight, which is always beneficial. A relaxed horse will always thrive much better than a highly strung one.

Feeding each horse as an individual is important. Some will require more protein, others more bulk; some may need wetter rations, whilst others would be better off with a supplement to help them 'do' well. Study each animal carefully and assess regularly what is required to keep the horse in top condition.

What to feed very much depends on what you are used to and on the individuals concerned. The following feedstuffs are those which have been found to be particularly useful for the show horse.

Barley is especially good for show horses because it is more fattening but less heating than oats, and is therefore very suitable for the horse that is likely to become overfresh. Micronised barley is preferred as it is clean and easily digested having been through a special heat process, which breaks down its hard exterior. It is also very good fed as a boiled feed mixed with a little linseed, which is excellent for the coat. To prepare this boiled feed, soak the barley and linseed together over-night and then put the whole lot in a slow oven during the day or bring to the boil and simmer gently for a couple of hours or until soft.

Any boiled food is more easily digested, and some people boil oats as well as barley. A mixture of oats and barley with linseed is extremely appetising. Some people give it with their mashes once or twice weekly, others feed it every day.

Oats can be a useful feed for those horses who lack sparkle in the ring, especially young animals and ridden four-year-olds, who easily tire.

There are now several specially made **coarse mixes** designed to suit horses in different types of work and these are becoming extremely popular. Choose a clean sweet-smelling variety which does not have too high a protein content. Some mixes look as if they've been thrown together with questionable ingredients, so go for a well-known brand that you feel you can rely on. Some mixes are specifically designed to be non-heating.

Sugar-beet pulp, well soaked for at least twelve hours, is excellent for fattening but should be used with caution as it has a very high energy content, so if your horse or pony is already rather flighty this should be cut down or kept to a minimum.

Bran and chaff make useful fillers but bran should only be used in moderation as it is now known to interfere with the balance of calcium and phosphorus if fed in large quantities. Bran mashes with Epsom salts twice a week are a good way of preventing a build-up of food and help to keep the show horse from becoming overfresh. Most chaff is now fed mixed with molasses in some form or other, which is excellent as an appetiser and high in all sorts of minerals, vitamins and trace elements. Molasses also comes in meal or syrup form, when it can be added to the feed or mixed with warm water to dampen it.

Maize is a very good fattening food which is not too heating. It is usually fed flaked and is found in most of the proprietary mixes.

Oil is most important in keeping the coat shiny and glossy and whilst there is adequate oil in most horse food, the addition of some-thing like cod liver oil is excellent for encouraging a little extra sheen.

SUGGESTIONS FOR FEEDING

	Breakfast	Lunch	Tea	Late
Broodmares and youngstock	stud cubes or oats/barley (micronised) or coarse mix (2–6 lbs/1–2.7 kg)	out by day	bran/chaff + stud cubes or coarse mix or oats/barley + boiled feed or sugar-beet (2–6 lbs/1–2.7 kg)	
Hacks, riding horses and light–framed horses	horse & pony cubes or micronised barley or coarse mix or Baileys (2–6 lbs/1–2.7 kg)	turn out for few hours	bran/chaff + horse & pony cubes or micronised barley/oats or coarse mix or Baileys + boiled food (2–4 lbs/1–1.8 kg)	coarse mix (2–3 lbs/1–1.3 kg) if necessary
Hunters, cobs and heavy built horses	stud cubes or Baileys or coarse mix (2–4 lbs/1–1.8 kg)	turn out	bran/chaff + horse & pony or stud cubes or barley/oats or Baileys or coarse mix + boiled barley or sugar-beet (2–6 lbs/1–2.7 kg)	stud cubes (2–4 lbs/1–8 kg)
Ponies	horse & pony cubes or Baileys or coarse mix (2 lbs/1 kg)	turn out	bran/chaff + horse & pony cubes or Baileys or coarse mix + sugar-beet (2 lbs/1 kg)	as breakfast (2 lbs/1 kg) if necessary

All animals to have bran mashes with Epsom salts once or twice weekly. Give extra boiled feed and cod liver oil in cold weather. Hay *ad lib* unless over–fat, then restrict. Feed supplements as required.

You might decide to feed some sort of **supplement** if you are doing a lot of showing. Choose one which seems right for your horse or stable and stick to it – don't become one of these people who give a mass of different supplements and extras, since most will either double up on the same ingredients causing an imbalance or simply be a waste of money. Some supplements are high in oil, so check this before feeding extra cod liver oil.

There are many excellent herbal supplements and remedies on the market, and these are very much in vogue. In fact they are nothing new – one's grandparents used to employ most of them as a matter of course. Nowadays, however, a little more scientific evidence exists to explain *why* they are so effective. One such remedy is garlic, well known as a 'cure-all' for coughs, colds and wind problems.

Good quality **hay** is particularly important and should make up between 60–70% approximately of the show horse's diet. Whether it is hard or soft hay matters little so long as it is of good quality, clean and sweet-smelling. Hay should be available all the time unless the horse has a tendency to get overfat.

Some horses have slight dust allergies and soaking the hay can be an easy way to overcome this problem. Alternatively, there are several varieties of vacuum-packed haylage available. Be careful to choose a mix which is not too high in energy as hay made this way retains more of its goodness than ordinary hay. Much smaller quantities should be fed.

Tasty trimmings from carrots, potatoes or chopped cabbages are often much appreciated and add variety to the diet. Freshly cut grass is also excellent, especially when it is not possible to turn the horse out.

The type of **water** your horse drinks can make quite a difference to its coat. Soft water definitely seems to impart an extra glossy and soft silky shine to the coat. Some people save rain water, both for the horse to drink and to wash it with. Of course, this is not always available when you want it but it is worth making the effort to save it. Be a little careful, however, if you are changing frequently from one type of drinking water to another as some horses have been known to show slight signs of colic.

Exercise

Turning out is an excellent way of providing exercise and relaxation. Used in this way it is just as important as riding and schooling, and by turning out, the danger of making the animal too fit is avoided. Most show animals would benefit from being ridden for half the week and turned out for the other half, or being ridden and then turned out for a few hours every day. Whether this is actually possible depends on the facilities available.

There is no substitute for a spell in the field each day. Many horses settle better if they have the company of a quiet friend. Make sure that the paddocks are well fenced and free from any hazards that could cause an injury.

The majority of horses love going out and if turned out regularly rarely gallop around recklessly. There are, however, some who are temperamentally unsuitable to be turned out as they fool about too much; these are best either ridden or lunged.

To protect against knocks and bruises while in the field, many people put on boots all round.

Lungeing is a useful way of exercising and can be done either loose on a lunge line and cavesson or as a proper work session with side reins attached to the bit. Many show horses tend to become very one-sided because they spend more time going round the show ring on the right rein, so lungeing provides an excellent opportunity for working them on the stiffer rein.

Youngsters from two-year-olds upwards can be lunged a little on either rein as part of their education, but this should not be overdone as circling is not good for a young animal's growing frame.

Long-reining is more appropriate and very good for all youngsters as there is no strain on any particular side of the body and it teaches them to go forward from the start, to accept the bit (which should be a simple rubber or kind rounded snaffle) and to get used to the roller. Those that have been well long-reined are little trouble when it comes to backing and breaking-in later on. They can be driven up and down tracks and round fields or schools so that half the hassle of getting them used to going out alone is already countered.

Long-reining can be used on all types of horses and ponies and may help their way of going when ridden, particularly those which do not go forward and tend to drop behind the bit.

All horses and ponies will require a certain amount of schooling relative to their intended classes, and for ridden horses this should be interspersed with hacking out.

Training and schooling is dealt with in the next chapter.

Long-reining is a very useful method of schooling young horses. It teaches them to go forward without a weight on their backs; it can also be a good way to correct faults in older horses. Youngsters that have been long-reined are generally easier to break-in and school later on.

Shoeing

Shoeing is most important, and how this is done may be reflected in how well and straight your horse moves. Regular checks on how your horse moves and attention by your farrier on a routine basis will pay dividends.

Lighter shoes may be necessary for the lighter types such as ponies, hacks and riding horses. These are often shod with aluminium plates to encourage them to have a lighter action but most other animals will be shown with light- to middleweight steel.

The farrier can often do a tremendous amount to help a horse with doubtful action and to disguise bad or odd-shaped feet. Talk over the options with him but be sure that a long-term effect is your ultimate aim – short cuts could be seriously detrimental to the horse.

Your farrier can also advise on the use of studs. Many show riders fit them to prevent slipping in the ring, especially in those classes where galloping is expected. Large studs are inadvisable on very hard ground.

Grooming

Grooming is another essential regular chore which will greatly influence the general appearance of the show horse. A well-groomed coat stands out, and although there is no doubt that some horses have especially good glossy coats without seeing a brush too often, the majority will benefit from a good daily grooming routine.

A **body brush** should be used all over. This should include the head and ears, as well as up between both front and hind legs and under the belly. Using the hand to rub round any sensitive areas, such as the ears, elbows and under the tummy, may be less ticklish to the sensitive horse.

A **rubber curry comb** is extremely efficient at loosening the hair once the coat is starting to change. Used in a circular motion it can be taken all over the body and is very helpful on both insides and outsides of the legs. The longer hairs on the legs often take quite a lot of effort to remove and may even require plucking out in some cases if they look unsightly and a show is imminent.

A **wisp** (nowadays many use the leather pad variety instead of the old hay type) may be necessary on animals that are not well developed on their necks and quarters. Strapping on a regular basis may help to enhance these areas but the secret lies in banging slowly, allowing time for the muscles to contract and then relax before the next bang. Done in this way the muscles are really made to work, but if the movement is too fast the correct effect is lost. Strapping should not be done on youngsters.

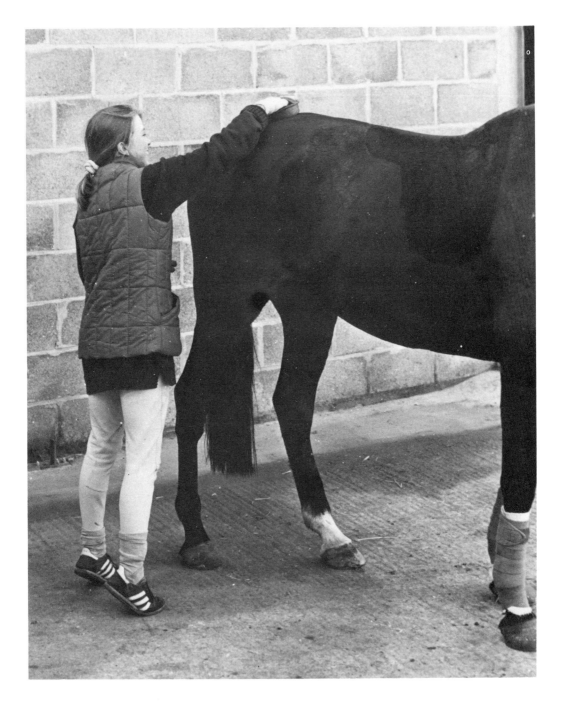

Strapping with a pad can help to build up weak muscles. Bang slowly on the long deep muscles of the quarters and the neck, on both sides, allowing time for the contraction and relaxation of the muscles to take place.

Care of the mane and tail comes into play during daily grooming, and damping and laying the mane over to the right side should be a part of the session. A good brush through, including the forelock, will encourage the mane to remain neat and tidy. The tail should be damped down well and a tail bandage applied for a few hours a day to ensure it stays looking good. Remember to remove the bandage before settling your horse for the night. Tail bandages must never be left on overnight.

An unruly mane can be improved by occasional plaiting over. It must be well damped first and should not be left plaited for more than twenty-four hours or the hairs will tend to break. 'Pull on' type hoods can be quite effective as mane layers so long as the mane is pushed well over to the right side underneath.

A lot depends on how well the mane and tail are pulled in the first place. If the tail is to be plaited the hairs should be as long as possible if it is to look really neat. Never brush out the ends of the tail as this can remove hairs and eventually ruin the appearance of the tail. Separate the hairs by hand if possible, or take hold of the tail firmly and brush out the ends on show days only.

A **sponge** should be used daily to clean round the eyes, nose and mouth to keep them fresh, and a separate sponge used on the dock and under the tail.

A **stable rubber** is the most important part of the grooming kit; use it to give the coat a final polish. If used every day after grooming it will help to keep the coat fine and remove particles of grease which come to the surface.

Hoof care should be carried out daily, with careful picking out of the hooves and a good oiling, inside and out, three or four times a week. Applications of cod liver oil are excellent for keeping the hooves in good condition. More conventional hoof oils can be used when the horse goes on an outing. Rub oil well into the coronet band to keep this in good condition, as it is from here that the foot grows. Any rough or torn bits of frog should be tidied up by your farrier.

The chestnuts on the horse's legs must be kept neat and tidy. These should be peeled off regularly and not allowed to grow too large. If they have become very tough and large your farrier will be able to pare them down to a manageable size; you can then keep them in good shape on a weekly basis when grooming.

Useful tips on general management

When considering the health, condition and day-to-day management of the show horse, the following points may help towards preventing unnecessary mistakes:

1. Feed the horse adequate food to keep condition on but do not overdo the energy intake so that it becomes unmanageable.

2. Give the horse adequate exercise to keep it calm and sensible. Do not overdo the work or it will become fitter and fitter and may get out of hand. Turn it out or loose lunge it occasionally to give it the chance to buck and kick and to relax.

3. Keep the animal well protected when out on exercise, especially if prone to knocks and bruises. Blemishes of any sort are not favoured in the show ring.

4. Make sure there is adequate bedding so the horse does not get scuffed or capped hocks when it rolls or lies down in its stable.

5. Teach the horse to lead and stand up properly from the word go, and be sure this is done properly when you lead it in and out of its stable. Practise standing it up, as if for the judge, two or three times a week.

6. All riding horses must be made to stand still while you mount and to remain standing until you ask them to move off. This way they are seen to be well mannered when mounted in the ring by the judge.

7. Make sure your show horse has been ridden by other people before allowing it into a show class where a judge is to ride. Some horses may have been ridden by just one person and it is unfair to the judge if he ends up being the one to discover that your horse does not take kindly to strangers. Some young horses may find the weight or size of different riders strange so do be sure to put a few different riders on top so that the youngster is not given any extra hassle at the show.

8. Plan your worming routine, shoeing and teeth care to suit your showing programme. It is inadvisable to have your animal shod the day before a show just in case the farrier has shod him a bit tight making him go a little uneven for a day or two. Have the shoeing done a few days beforehand to allow time for any problem to settle down.

CHAPTER · 3

TRAINING AND SCHOOLING

The training of the show horse or pony is vital to its success. No judge has time to waste standing around waiting for your exhibit to show itself off properly. What the judge wants to see is your horse's best performance, and straightaway, whether the animal is being led in-hand or ridden. Any exhibit that fails to please at the moment when it has the judge's attention is liable to be ignored, however perfect its conformation. It is therefore up to the exhibitor to present the horse in front of the judge in such a way that a favourable assessment can be made.

Requirements for in-hand classes

Leading – in-hand classes are difficult enough to judge at the best of times so it goes without saying that your horse must lead properly. You should walk at its shoulder and the horse must walk forward well, keeping its head straight so that its movement is not spoiled as you attempt to pull its head round to control it. This can produce a very uneven walk, giving the appearance of lameness.

While some horses can be led in a neat headcollar it is usual for broodmares to be led in a double bridle, stallions in an in-hand show bridle with a snaffle, and youngstock the same but often with a little rubber bit or a neat show cavesson. A coupling and leather or white-webbed lead rein are most appropriate. Heavy horses are often shown in halters as are some of the native breeds. The emphasis must be on control first and foremost. The charts in the second section outline the normal tack used for each type of class. Make sure that you practise at home and are confident that your horse is controllable in the tack you intend to use at the show.

Some stallions can become a bit of a handful at a show, or just not show themselves off too well, without side reins. These are quite acceptable in most cases and will keep the horse's head straight so that it will move well. Practise running up in-hand with side reins on, ensuring that they are only so tight as to keep the horse under control and in no way restrict it or pull its head in so that it is unable to show itself off to its best advantage.

Giving a good impression when running up in-hand is very important if you are to catch the judge's eye. A well-behaved exhibit and neatly turned-out handler look professional and demand attention.

Foals must be led properly and should be kept close to their mothers. They must learn to stand still whilst the dam is walked and trotted back in-hand. They must also learn to be walked up and trotted back quietly beside the dam. Straightness is what is being looked for when the judge asks for a trot up, so try to ensure that all animals, regardless of age or size, go straight – this is the first and most important lesson to be learnt.

Standing the horse up in-hand is the most important moment in the class so practise thoroughly at home, teaching the horse to move into position quickly and to stand up well. While some breeds require a particular stance most classes call for the animal to stand so that the judges can just see all four legs. The horse should stand naturally, being neither too stretched out nor too 'bunched' together, and straight when viewed from the back or front.

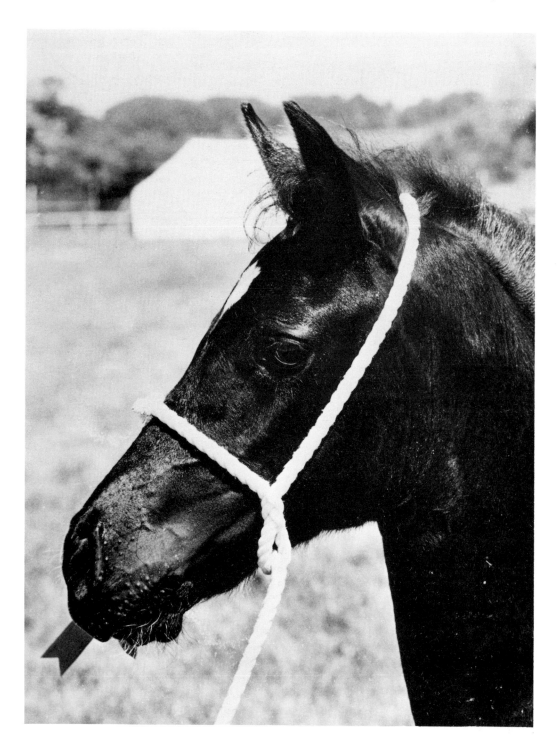

Knowing how to make your horse stand up well will pay dividends when it comes to having to do so in front of the judge. Regular practice at home is the key; you can also experiment with tack and plaiting so that you know exactly what will suit your particular horse on the big day.

LEFT *This foal has the look of a future champion. Ears pricked, oozing presence, with an eye-catching star, it cannot fail to be noticed.*

The neck should be nicely arched at a suitable height to make the horse's head and general bearing look its best. The ears should be pricked to complete a good picture from which the judge can make his choice. Picking up a handful of grass in the ring may produce the desired effect on the day, but don't practise this routine at home too much or it may lose its impact.

Ensure that your animal responds quickly to being pulled forward or pushed back a step so that it is in the right position when the judge inspects it, and also that it leads away straight and turns away from you when you turn to trot back straight. Don't allow it to misbehave or become out of control; likewise be sure it is not idle, having to be dragged along.

Requirements for ridden classes

The ridden horse must be perfectly mannered in every way. It is no good practising by yourself at home – you must be sure to ride it in company quite regularly so that you know it will behave at a show. Make certain it is used to other horses overtaking quite close and will, above all, not kick out. Children's ponies must be well behaved in all respects but particularly when other ponies are coming up close behind, as children are notoriously bad about looking where they are going. Ponies should be forward-going and obedient but in no way strong for the child. Leading-rein ponies should be manoeuvred as much as possible by the child with very little help from the handler. They should show willingness and active responses while in no way being too jerky and quick nor sluggish.

Regular schooling is important if the horse is to go well in the ring and give the judge a good ride. This working hunter is learning to accept the double bridle quite happily and is being ridden by a different rider to ensure that he will be unworried when ridden by a judge in the ring for the very first time.

Hacks and riding horses must be beautifully schooled showing collection and extension, halt, rein back, strike-offs on a given leg and the latter must be able to gallop.

Hunters and cobs must be good workmanlike rides going forward into the bridle well, comfortable on both reins and really able to stretch out and gallop. They must pull up well, halt and stand still.

Ridden native ponies and riding pony stallions etc. must go nicely at all paces, be comfortable and obedient and be well schooled. Even a Shetland, if well trained, can be a lovely ride, despite its size. Ponies tend to be a bit 'mouthy' probably because they are apt to be ridden by children who tend to treat them a bit like a toy and pull away at their mouths. It is worth spending a little time in finding the best bit and schooling the animal carefully before entering a class.

Training the rider is just as important as training the horse, as ultimately it is very much up to the rider to show off the horse. When schooling the horse it is worth making the rider do a show periodically and having a practice in a field with other horses. For horses or ponies that are going to be ridden by the judge this is a good time to practise putting other riders on board.

Children need to be taught how to ride an individual show and must learn not to ride too close or too far away from the judges. They must be taught as much as possible, but not to the point where the lessons become a bore. This is very important if the younger generation are to enjoy themselves and continue showing.

Jumping – working hunters and working hunter ponies, which will be required to jump a course of fences, must be trained up to the necessary standard. Most of these courses are rustic and some include a combination fence which involves a turn for the second element.

Far too often one sees horses and ponies coming unstuck in these classes due to insufficient training. Be quite sure that you have thoroughly trained the animal so that it can jump a reasonable grid, will go well round a cross-country course and is confident over a set of show jumps. Equipped with this sort of all-round experience most animals should be capable of jumping the average working hunter course. In case a ditch or some form of water jump is included in the course, plenty of practice over these types of fence is recommended. Working hunter courses should be jumped at a fair hunting pace, and a good flowing round is expected. Too often problems arise because riders will not get straight at the fences and give the horses the best chance, so this must be instilled into the jockey.

Galloping plays an important part, especially in hunter classes, but riders very often hold their horses back instead of really letting the judge see how they can move. While galloping is not something one should overdo it is up to the rider to show that the horse can stride out

well. Sit up and ride the horse forward in front of you, then pull it up. The horse will look its best galloping with its head up and out a little, and it should look and be controlled throughout. At home practise on both reins as the judge might want to ride the gallop in both directions so the horse should be equally handy on the right and left leg. Working the horse quietly then asking for a good strong pace, riding it forward in front of you, then coming back to a collected pace and riding it on again, is good training. Do not always practise your gallop in the same place but vary it so that the horse does not start to recognise a certain spot as being a cue to gallop.

The **walk** is the pace that the horse shows during the final parade round before being pulled into place, so it is worth spending time on this to ensure that your horse or pony looks good and walks out well. A horse with a stilted and restricted pace will not be favoured any more than one that is slopping along with its head on the floor. Look at the horse yourself or ask a knowledgeable assistant to watch you ride the horse to see how it looks its best. A good rhythm and flowing stride should be the aim with the head being well carried and the horse in self-balance.

The **halt** needs regular practice. Neither the rider nor judge (if appropriate) will appreciate having to haul away at the horse in an effort to stop it. Schooling should be such that the horse responds immediately and can come back to a halt when required from any pace, including gallop. It must then stand still and remain so, even if the rider decides to drop the reins on the neck, until asked to move forward. This is most important as it is often the way a judge might assess manners in the class. Being unwilling to halt and stand still may well prove the deciding factor in the final placings.

Mounting and dismounting are other times when manners may be observed, and, here again, the horse must remain still. It is absolutely essential to teach the horse to stand and be obedient from the very beginning. Many professionals train their horses to stand still by themselves to impress the judges. It is not difficult to do this if you are consistent in your training and make the effort to insist that your horse stands still whenever you ask, and that you mount and dismount observing the same rule. Remember, the horse is a creature of habit and will learn quite quickly providing that you enforce the habit every

OPPOSITE ABOVE *For the horse that is required to jump, it is essential that it has been well schooled and given good basic training at home before attempting a fence in public. In some performance classes horses are now expected to jump simple fences from an early age. This horse is jumping on the lunge in a performance class for youngsters in Ireland.*

OPPOSITE BELOW *Galloping can win or lose the class, so make sure you put on a good performance when required. Vin Toulson always has his horses beautifully balanced and can really show off a gallop to advantage.*

39

time, using the same words to indicate your wishes, such as 'whoa' or 'stand still'. Practise mounting from the ground as well as being given a leg up so that the horse is accustomed to both methods.

Reining back is usually required in show pony classes, and for hacks and riding horses. It is an indication of good training, so spend some time perfecting it. The animal should step back straight with lightness and ease and the rider should not be seen to pull to achieve a response. Correct training will be required to show this important movement, and very often it is followed by a strike-off into canter, accentuating the degree of training reached. It is best not to rein back at all until your horse is sufficiently well schooled and likewise not to attempt it on a young horse until it is well settled in the ring. Timing is always one of the secrets of success and to ask for a rein back when the animal's eyes are almost out on stalks at its first show will probably result in the reaction such stupidity deserves. Practise at home first, then try out your training at a small show first before taking the plunge in front of all the stars. In showing, it is better not to attempt a particular movement at all than to perform it badly.

All training for the show ring should aim to produce nice rhythmic paces and total obedience. The show animal must not spook or misbehave in any way so it makes sense to take it on frequent outings and ride it about to see the sights so that it becomes quite used to all the varied and often quite alarming sights of the show world.

If you can enter a **variety** of different classes so much the better, as this will help check any desire to anticipate the usual pattern of a certain class. Many animals learn the routine of walk, trot, canter and tend to get strong in readiness for the gallop. Attempting something different, such as a dressage test, which any well-schooled show horse should be more than capable of, will vary the scene a little. Side-saddle, which is becoming so popular again, may well offer another outlet for your horse's talents, as may equitation classes, whose format, being different to the usual show classes, can be useful as a variation even if you do not wish to compete in them seriously.

Side-saddle is something that also requires practice at home. While it is usually unnecessary to do this too often, both horse and rider will benefit from a few schools to perfect the way of going. Check that the saddle is a good fit and remains so. Sometimes side-saddles need restufffing if the horse has put on or lost a lot of weight or muscle on its back since the previous year. The rider must be sure to sit up straight and the horse should go forward straight and respond to the rider's aids quite happily, despite the right leg not being there. It may be necessary to sharpen up the horse's responses on this side by using a long dressage whip so that it learns to understand that the whip is taking the place of the leg. Be sure to take care of the horse's back and harden it up with surgical spirit or lead lotion if necessary. If the rider is sitting correctly and the saddle fits properly there is rarely a problem. Depending on whether you are doing ladies' hacks, hunters or side-saddle on ponies, practise until you have the horse going just as it should in all paces.

Loading and travelling

One aspect of training that must never be forgotten is ensuring that your show animal will load into the horsebox or trailer. Nothing is more frustrating than a horse who will not go in. Most starts for shows are inevitably quite early and the last thing you want to discover when you are perhaps pushed for time at the first show of the season, is that you have failed to check up on this important item of training.

Youngsters, in particular, should be made to go in and out of the box periodically, and if difficult, given their feeds inside until they are confident and happy about it. A couple of trial runs are sensible also, to be certain you are not going to have problems on the big occasion.

Protect the show horse well, particularly over knees, hocks and tail which are all vulnerable to injury on the journey. Big knees, capped hocks and a badly rubbed tail are certainly going to wreck the show horse's appearance, quite apart from reducing its value.

Most animals will settle quite quickly as long as they have some hay to nibble at, but there are a few who are rather neurotic about being cooped up in a horsebox. One way of treating these is to let them spend a day in it well padded up. They must learn to accept it at some stage, and the sooner the better. Be careful with any who may start trying to climb out, and never leave them with a haynet or unattended in case they get themselves into trouble. Maddening as it may be, per-severance is what matters, so if you set aside a few mornings to sort out the animal your day at the show will be so much more pleasant.

Some animals get quite desperate if left looking out on the surround-ing scene and try (and some have succeeded) to jump out of the horsebox. To start with, it is best to keep the box shut up unless you can be with them, but this is normally a short-lived problem and as the animal has more outings it tends to settle down quite quickly.

Taking another experienced horse along for company to the first couple of shows can be worthwhile, remembering to take the young-ster out of the box first, so that it doesn't become hysterical, thinking it has lost its friend. Loading the schoolmaster first will also give confi-dence to the youngster.

Firm and sensible handling is required for it is so important that your horse is a pleasure to take around rather than a menace, so tackle this part of the training early and overcome any problem before it escalates.

A poll guard is a sensible precaution for travelling a very big horse or a youngster liable to play up when in the box.

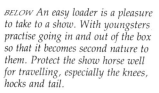

BELOW An easy loader is a pleasure to take to a show. With youngsters practise going in and out of the box so that it becomes second nature to them. Protect the show horse well for travelling, especially the knees, hocks and tail.

What not to do when training the show animal

Above all, the show horse or pony must enjoy its work so that it 'shows off' to the judge and looks happy with its ears pricked. If you ever lose this look you have basically lost your show horse so it is so important not to overdo showing. Sourness can set in if the animal is dragged around from show to show with no other variety in its life except training and showing. This may also lead to anticipation in the ring so that the horse tries to take over instead of only performing as and when asked.

Never overfeed your horse so that it becomes overloaded and gross, which can easily undermine its health and lead to such problems as curbs, splints and thoroughpins, as well as impairing wind or even the heart, not to mention the many other constitutional problems which tend to arise if the horse becomes overfat.

Make quite sure the horse is well protected throughout his training so that he does not knock himself and become blemished, and protect him well when travelling.

Never allow bad habits to set in. The horse must behave all the time and any misbehaviour must be treated firmly straightaway so that it does not develop into a problem. Horses, and particularly ponies, learn bad habits just as quickly if not quicker than good ones so *never* allow them to get the upper hand at any time. At the slightest indication of any problem treat the cause immediately. Nappiness, coming out of the line, kicking out at others, behaving badly and not standing in line, must all be dealt with either with a sharp reprimand or extra work, with each horse being treated according to what would be best for its character. The secret is to nip the problem in the bud.

Youngstock must be well trained at home but, despite training, can be quite naughty at the scene of the show. These animals really do need firmly controlling at all times as they can easily become a danger to the public as well as to you and to themselves. They are seldom much trouble so long as you make it quite clear from the start that you are the boss. Failure do to this may mean you end up with a raving lunatic who becomes a liability.

With all training make quite sure you know what you are aiming for. Watch the professionals, see how they do things, then perfect the art at home in readiness for the big occasion.

CHAPTER · 4

RINGCRAFT

Ridden classes

The art of riding your show horse in the ring and showing it off to its best advantage is something that can only be learnt through experience, but there are several points which should be thought about before you start.

The first is learning to make the most of your show ring. Some are better than others, but the number in the class can make a tremendous difference and coping with large numbers in a small ring can definitely be a problem at times.

Riding in the ring

Keep an eye on the judge to see where he is looking – this is the place where you want to make sure you have a clear space for yourself to show off your horse. Work out if you need to cut a corner to fit into a clear slot or whether you want to pull out into the corners of the ring to let a bunch of riders pass. Sometimes it may be necessary to ride a discreet small circle at the back of the ring to manoeuvre into a good position.

You should already have worked out at home how best to ride your horse in front of the judge, but generally you want the horse to be going freely forward on the bit without looking restricted or becoming over-bent and on its forehand. A good head carriage is very important. The walk should be free and regular. The trot should demonstrate the elasticity and movement of the horse, being unrestricted and well balanced, whether in working or extended trot. The canter should be relaxed and flowing, ridden in the manner required for the type of class in which you are riding.

Galloping must be controlled and is generally only performed down one long side in front of the judge. It is therefore important that you make the most of this occasion as, particularly with hunters and cobs, if the judge doesn't see your horse gallop he will not consider you worthy of a high place.

Creating a good impression in front of the judge is vital – and the earlier you start, the sooner you will become an expert. This child is looking confident on her beautifully turned-out pony and Mum is leaving the lead rein quite loose, showing the pony's manners off to best advantage.

The horse should be balanced on the corner and then asked to gallop on, well past the judge. Take care that the horse does not slip at the corner – in fact, it would be prudent to put in studs if the ring is small or the going is particularly slippery. If you feel your horse needs help, discuss the matter with your farrier but, generally, a well-balanced horse should be able to pull up and not lose its footing.

Be sure that you can pull up your horse with ease and, particularly with children's ponies, be quite certain that the rider has full control even though the smaller ones only gallop singly. Check your curb chain. Some classes are asked to change the rein, and if you know your horse does this well, then do your change in front of the judge, if not, change either before or well afterwards.

Nearly all classes are shown on the right rein which often means that horses get a little stiff on the left, so practise on the left, particularly with ridden horses that are to be ridden by the judge, so that the horse goes equally well in either direction.

The final walk round is a fairly critical time as this is the occasion, particularly if the class has galloped, that manners may show up, with some horses not settling and walking properly. Be sure to relax yourself at this time, a few deep breaths may well help the two of you to remain calm. Don't let your horse become idle; keep it walking up to the bit and attentive all the time. Don't look directly at the judge but watch out of the corner of your eye to see if you have been called in – many are the times a rider has failed to notice and then been missed out altogether, ending up much further down the line.

The individual show

If you have to do a show it should be short and sharp and give a really good impression of how your horse is trained. The walk, trot and canter, showing a change of rein, striding on, or a gallop as appropriate, a halt, rein back and a stand still on a loose rein will show all the judge needs to see. How you do this is up to you, but the shorter the better. It does not take long for an experienced judge to assess a well-trained horse so remember that 'short is beautiful' as far as your show is concerned. The judge will take into account obedience, way of going, and acceptance of the rider and bridle.

Riding by the judge

When your horse is to be ridden by the judge, quickly ensure that the leathers are approximately the correct length and then sit and pray that the animal reflects the hours of work and training you have put in and gives the judge a good ride. Be certain to keep the horse warm before and after it is ridden so that it does not get a cold back and its coat stays looking good. Put a sheet over him if it is very hot.

Don't be disappointed if the judge stays on board for a very short time. He may have a lot of others to ride and usually has an impossibly short time in which to judge the class. If he obtains a good feel straightaway and likes the horse he will not waste further time on it. Of course, if he doesn't like it at all he may also get off as soon as possible, so you may be none the wiser either way. The important things from your point of view are that the animal behaves and does not let you down and that it goes calmly and obediently.

Running up in-hand

When the horse is stripped and has to stand up in front of the judge, here again your rehearsals at home should pay off. Make sure your groom has quickly flicked off any saddle or sweat marks and be ready to walk up as the last horse in front of you is being shown. Stand the horse a little away from the judge on (if possible) a flat piece of ground and stand in front of the animal holding its reins, which should not drag on the ground. Smile at the judge and answer any questions briefly as you quickly check the horse is standing up properly. Pluck a little grass to encourage him to prick his ears and arch his neck. If the

Showing the horse off, in-hand, in front of the judge, is quite an art. Robert Oliver has his cob standing beautifully with each leg visible and the horse in balance. The ears can be encouraged forward with a discreet titbit of grass or a Polo mint carried in the pocket. Remember to run the horse up close to the judge so that he or she does not have to chase round to see how straight your horse moves.

judge moves round to view from the other side push him back a pace if necessary and then lead him up at the walk, push him away from you to turn, and then trot *straight* back towards and on past the judge so that he can see its action. If you have a slightly doubtful mover, the clever rider may move on past in a curve to help disguise this shortcoming.

In certain classes movement can play a very important part and handlers of heavy horses, Welsh cobs, etc. need to be able to run fast to show their horses properly in-hand. If you can't do this yourself make sure you have a suitable person ready to lead on these occasions. Always be sure you know what stance is required for the different classes and teach your horse or pony to stand accordingly. This is only necessary for a few, but to be professional you must produce the required goods.

Side-saddle

For side-saddle classes, whether ponies, hacks, hunters, etc., make sure your helper is in the ring early enough to help you dismount.

TOP Running up in-hand requires a speedy pair of legs when it comes to such breeds as the Welsh Cob (Section D). Sensible but neat running shoes are essential. This lovely cob is being helped to maintain straightness through the use of an in-hand roller and side reins.

BOTTOM This ladies' hunter looks to be a lovely ride, even if a little on its forehand at this particular moment. The side-saddle horse should be beautifully schooled and a comfortable and smooth ride, with the jockey immaculately turned out.

Remove the elastic from around the toe, which keeps the skirt down in place, and then ensure the skirt is folded round the back to become an apron and buttoned under the jacket looking neat and tidy. Adjust the stirrup to suit the judge if appropriate.

When remounting, be sure to tighten girths correctly and don't rush this important part of tacking up, even if the rest of the class is waiting; however, be as quick as you can.

General tips on ringcraft

When riding in the ring, don't fall into any of the undermentioned traps, which tend to catch the unwary.

Never get into a bunch, especially not in front of the judge. If you keep your wits about you it is quite possible to avoid this situation by using the ring sensibly.

Be careful of the unsporting competitor who will come on your inside just as you are about to trot beautifully in front of the judge – there are unfortunately several around.

Sit up, look professional and really show your horse off at all times. Tipping forward with your head poked down hardly presents a pleasing picture; also the horse will tend to go the same way as you will push it onto its forehand riding like this.

Carry your show cane in the middle so that it is nicely balanced in your hand. In hack classes it is quite permissible and an indication of

Children invariably fail to notice when they are getting into the wrong position and often end up in a bunch. It does, of course, take time for them to learn what is required.

good manners and training to ride with one hand, resting the end of your cane on your knee. If carrying a hunting crop be sure that you hold this so that the head is facing down. The leather thong must have a lash on the end. In side-saddle classes longer whips are permitted. If you are not using a show cane it is correct to hold a cutting or neat dressage whip up at the top.

When galloping sit up well and ride the horse strongly forward in front of the judge. Don't be one of the nervous types who won't let the horse go. Avoid being overtaken – this is the time when horses play up.

Don't go too close to other horses; some may be at their first show and quite unpredictable. Treat every horse with suspicion and you are then likely to avoid an unnecessary kick.

Look at the horses in the collecting ring and if possible avoid following the most outstanding horse when actually in the ring as it will only overshadow your own. If you feel you have the best horse, try to enter the ring first if you are confident your horse will walk round quietly. First impressions are important so get out there, assert your position and don't hold back. If you can't go in first then coming in last is another good idea, so long as there are not too many in the class. Wherever you go, make quite sure you are seen by the judge.

Try to avoid getting stuck behind a horse that is misbehaving; give it a wide berth so that it does not upset your own mount, and find another slot.

If your horse is rather spooky or nervous, don't go too close to the outside of the ring where there tend to be all sorts of hazards and distractions. Stay just on the inside so that it will be more relaxed.

If the going is bad, study the ring on your first walk round and try to avoid any deep or rock-hard patches with no cover which might be slippery, especially if you are required to gallop.

Sometimes young horses get quite fidgety when standing in line for long stints. It may be best to dismount. Playing with the bit or taking a packet of Polos into the ring will probably help. Nibbles of grass can be a last resort, but this is a bit of a give-away and the resulting green slobber tends to get everywhere and looks unsightly.

It looks extremely unprofessional to be seen smoking in the ring and is the height of rudeness to the judge. Likewise, wandering up and down the line chatting to friends is equally disgraceful. If you have other exhibits in the ring then discreetly walking down the back of the line is one thing, but if possible send your groom instead.

You should stand beside your horse while dismounted during the class and your groom should stand quietly behind the horse once he or she has finished tidying it up. The less that is seen to be done the better it looks, and generally the more relaxed the horse will be.

In-hand classes

For in-hand classes the exhibits must be well behaved at all times, but with several youngsters perhaps on their first outing this is not always easy to achieve. Some good exercise the day before is a wise precaution as any equine playing about is a danger not only to the public but to you and itself as well. Keep your exhibit occupied and under control.

Be certain that the leader or handler is experienced and strong enough to cope with a youngster. A docile broodmare is one thing, her exuberant one-, two- or three-year-old quite another. The well-behaved foal may be quite a different animal with its new-found independence and strength a year later. It really is essential to ensure that all in-hand horses or ponies can be adequately controlled.

Neatness and tidiness in the ring for both horse and leader is a must; sloppy jeans, tee-shirts, frilly dresses, etc. are not the right gear for the show ring. On seeing such clothing most judges will automatically tend to assume that anyone wearing such unprofessional attire is hardly likely to have a decent exhibit anyway. Suitable footwear which allows you to run up your horse, is an important item, and a show cane must always be carried.

Well-grown foals and youngstock can be very strong so it is important that their handlers are able to control them if they become playful or excited. Although the handler shown is very neatly turned out, a show cane should have been carried.

Standing in line can be a little unnerving with some youngsters or stallions, so keep an eye on your animal all the time. Don't stand too close to others and if you have any problems be firm straight away. It is usually lack of discipline that is the only problem as so many people will not teach their horses to behave and respect their handlers at an early age. A pathetic tap on the nose does nothing except encourage the animal to snap back like a spoilt child. A really hard rap given immediately the horse does anything wrong, and only then, is what is required.

With stallions and colts keep a discreet eye out to ensure their sheaths are not showing. If a colt draws in line walk him around at the back until he settles. Don't allow him to run round in circles but keep him occupied in some way. If in mixed classes you find your colt next to a filly, stand him a little in front and keep his attention throughout so that he does not get bored and naughty.

It is not difficult to keep colts and stallions under control if you are observant and command their respect. Those who do not have their animals under control should not be handling them anyway. They and their animals are a danger to everyone.

The grand parade of prize-winners can be quite an awe-inspiring spectacle, with so many horses, ponies and youngsters in the ring. In such situations it becomes even more vital for handlers to keep their wits about them.

The role of the groom

Grooms should take as little as possible into the ring, but a sponge, stable rubber, body brush, hoof pick and show sheet, depending on the weather, are the bare essentials.

In very hot weather the horse's coat will tend to stand up so a sheet should be placed over the animal; in cold weather the same may happen as the horse tends to get chilled while standing in line. A day rug will keep the horse warm and should be put on as soon as possible.

Grooms are usually allowed into the ring after the exhibits have been lined up. They should stand quietly behind their horses and only do

The groom should be neatly turned out for the ring. He or she should just bring the essentials: i.e. body brush, stable rubber, hoof pick, sponge, and an oiled hoof brush if appropriate. It should not be necessary to bring in anything more, except perhaps a smart rug or sheet, plus waterproofs if wet.

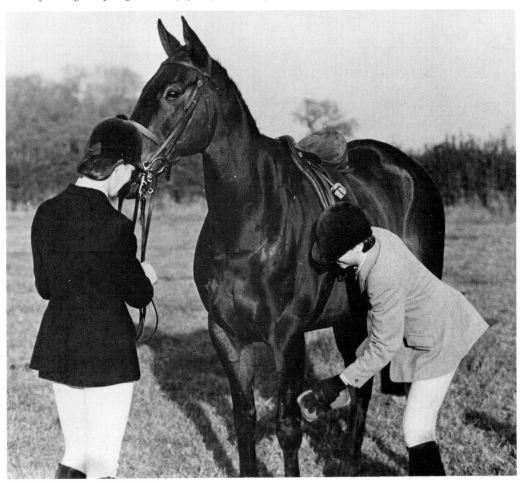

the minimum. They should not be seen giving the horse a full-scale grooming session in the ring, but rather should quickly tidy up as necessary. Too much fiddling around will often upset the horse and may start to make it misbehave. In ridden classes the groom or rider must alter the stirrup length to suit the judge, so the steward should be asked at what length the judge likes to ride.

Once all the exhibits have been seen by the judge the groom should leave the ring at the back of the line as unobtrusively as possible. Grooms should also enter this way, being sure not to get in the way of anyone performing a show.

Watch the professionals

When at a show, take every opportunity to learn from what you see. Look at those at the top of the line, and then at those at the bottom. Try to glean as much as possible about the requirements for that particular class. Look at how the professionals are turned out; notice what tack is used and how the horses are trained. The most professional people are seen to do very little but manage to have their exhibits looking just right; without appearing flashy they look the part, being neat in every respect, well presented and well behaved, and stand out as looking very worthy winners. Try to follow their example.

CHAPTER · 5

FORMALITIES

Registrations, memberships and certificates

Although many people have good fun entering classes at small local shows, the serious-minded will have to register their animals with the relevant breed society or association which governs the rules and regulations for that particular breed or type of class.

It is usual for both the exhibitor and horse to be registered, as well as the rider, annually. This will involve filling in an identification form and, where relevant, a Joint Measurement Scheme certificate may be required as proof of the animal's height. Make sure you get this done in plenty of time and arrange this with your veterinary surgeon. Only an approved vet may carry out the measurement.

Membership and registration numbers often have to be quoted on entry forms so it is important that you think about this early enough not to miss out on those early shows. Most societies run their memberships from 1 January. If your horse or pony is registered with several societies keep your record carefully and take a photocopy with you to shows, in case of any query on eligibility for a class or special rosette.

Flu vaccinations

Nearly all shows now require a valid certificate of flu vaccination. This is another item which requires forward planning and the current procedure is as follows: two primary doses must be given within the stipulated period (between 28 and 92 days) before the horse may compete, then a third dose is required between 150 and 215 days, and an annual booster thereafter. The vet should sign *and* stamp the certificate, which should be of the diagrammatic type undeniably relating to that particular horse. Its details should be currently recorded. Many shows insist on seeing this certificate or a photocopy before accepting your entry so it is worth having a few photocopies run off to send or take with you to the show.

Don't leave checking your flu vaccinations until it is too late and always make a note of when boosters are due so that you don't miss the date and have to start the whole procedure again.

Entries

When making entries, do be sure to read all the details concerning your classes. Some schedules are more than a little confusing and entry forms likewise. Some class numbers are subdivided into groups, especially in youngstock classes, so be sure you have put yours into the right section for its age, height, etc. Write clearly and legibly so that the details appear correctly in the catalogue, and put in as much information as you can on breeding, breeder, age, colour, etc. so that those watching can get as much out of the class as possible. Check if any arm bands need to be worn to show that you are eligible for special awards, and put this down on your entry form if required. Enclose any necessary details regarding memberships or registration numbers for the current year and copies of vaccination certificates. Avoid sending the originals as if they get lost this can cause problems. Send the correct amount in entry fees, and for stabling if required.

Filling in entry forms, sending off for schedules, checking that memberships and horse registrations are valid, are some of the necessary formalities which have to be fitted in at the start of the season. Remember that flu vaccinations and height certificates may be required, especially at the larger shows.

Keep a note in your show entry book of exactly what you have requested with stabling, along with your list of entries. Always ask for sufficient passes. Some shows are notoriously stingy about this and you can do without the hassle of arriving with three people and only two passes. It is usually only the bigger shows that check their attendances rather thoroughly that require passes. Some shows require a stamped self-addressed envelope for the return of numbers and passes, so be sure to supply one if this is the case. At other shows you may have to collect your numbers from the secretary on arrival, so give yourself adequate time as occasionally there is quite a queue before the first class of the day. Don't forget to take with you all the show information and numbers if these have been sent out in advance.

CHAPTER · 6

DRESSING FOR THE SHOW RING

Having the right tack and clothes is essential if you want to look professional in the show ring. Remember, it is the animal that is being judged, not you; your clothes should be neat, tidy and well fitting, and, above all they should not detract from the horse.

Clothes for the rider

What you wear depends on the class being judged and guidelines for each type of class are given in the charts at the back of the book. It is considered very unprofessional not to be seen wearing the correct clothes for the class, and even worse if you over-dress, so study the form carefully and ensure that you are properly attired.

Neatness and tidiness are the two most important factors. Collars and ties should look and be neat with a tie-pin securing everything in place. Some people fasten the points of their collars with a tie-pin for added neatness. If hunting ties (or stocks) are to be worn they should be well tied and not too bulky. They should be secured with a plain stock pin and large safety pins to keep the ends in place to prevent them coming out. The stock pin should be worn straight across horizontally unless it has a small figure on it, in which case it can be placed diagonally. It is both incorrect and dangerous for the pin to be worn vertically.

Children's jodhpurs should be a good fit, with elastic sewn into the bottoms so that they stay neatly down over the jodhpur boots. They should be a good neutral beige or cream colour and not too bright for working ponies.

Breeches should be well fitting, and for hunters and cobs a neutral beige colour. Cream is usual for the more showy classes, such as for hacks, riding horses and ponies.

Hunting boots should be a good fit and not too short in the leg. They should be beautifully polished so that they have a shine worthy of the work that has gone into the horse. Garter straps should always be worn. As most modern breeches no longer have buttons sewn just below the knee, these should be sewn on and the garter strap slotted in between.

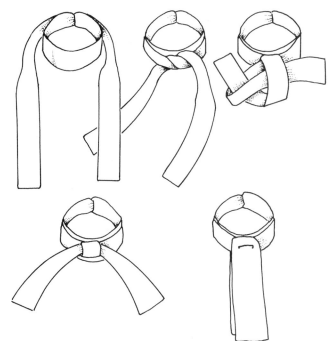

ABOVE Cobs and their riders correctly and neatly turned out. The riders are in ratcatcher dress, which is appropriate for morning or county shows (as for hunters). The horses are wearing plain tack with plain browbands.

Tying a hunting tie. A neat end-result with the knot well-covered and a plain stock pin placed horizontally (never vertically) is correct.

Garter straps should be placed between the top two buttons on breeches, with the buckle just to the outside. Spurs should always be worn with long boots, except by judges.

BELOW For pure-bred mountain and moorland classes tweed coats are worn. The ponies are left natural but would have to be plaited up if entered for ordinary working hunter or other classes.

Jodhpur boots, usually worn by younger children, may be black or brown but must be spotlessly clean.

Spurs should always be worn with hunting boots. The curve of the spur must point downwards and the spur-strap buckle should be on the outside of the boot with the point of the strap pointing downwards. Both spur and buckle should be polished. In children's classes spurs are not permitted.

The coat should be neat and tidy and fit well. It should not be too short in the body or in the sleeves, though this is more understandable with growing children. Tweed jackets should be unobtrusive without a strikingly obvious pattern or check. Two or three buttons at the front and the same on the opening of the lower arm are correct. Black or navy blue jackets (brown is acceptable for children) should be well fitting with no obvious or bright-coloured lining. If a buttonhole is worn it should be small and neat and on no account too large or effusive.

Hunting caps should be black or navy blue (brown if a brown jacket is worn) and worn so that the peak is horizontal to the ground. Hair should be neatly tied back or plaited for girls, and neatly tucked away in a hairnet for ladies. It is very incorrect to have hair coming out under the brim of a hat or to have the hat placed on the back of the head. Earrings are also inappropriate.

Bowlers should also be worn square to the ground, and ladies should have a neat bun at the back. Bowlers can be quite correct for both men and women but should be worn with a collar and tie and a tweed coat; they are also seen with black and blue coats for side-saddle riding, and worn with a veil.

Top hats are only worn for finals or in evening show classes. A hunting tie is always worn with a top hat, and for ladies, a veil is used with a top hat for side-saddle classes. For women it is correct to wear a bun, false if necessary, with a top hat.

At Royal shows in the afternoon, or evenings for finals and championships, correct hunting attire is worn for hunter and cob classes. The correct dress for men is a plain or cut-away black or scarlet hunting coat, top hat, hunting tie, with white breeches and top boots with white garters for a scarlet coat, or beige breeches and plain boots for a black coat. For women, plain blue or black coat, fawn breeches, plain hunting boots, hunting tie and top hat are appropriate. A hunting whip should be carried and, as always, spurs should be worn with long boots.

For evening wear in hack classes, the frock coat, overalls and top hats are still worn by men for finals and championships at major shows, accentuating the elegance of this type of horse. Women wear top hats and blue or black cut-away coats.

David Tatlow demonstrates the correct dress for hunter classes in the evening, for finals and championships, and at Royal shows: top hat, scarlet or black plain or cut-away coat, white breeches, top boots with white garters and hunting whip.

Gloves should be worn at all times. Pale string gloves should be worn with full hunting dress and are equally correct with a tweed coat. Dark brown leather gloves are worn with tweed and blue or black coats and for side-saddle riding.

The show cane, either Malacca or leather-covered, is carried for all show classes and should be a comfortable size, length and thickness for the person using it. It should not be longer than 32 ins (81 cm) and is usually shorter.

Clothes for the handler

As for all showing, the handler must be as neat, tidy and well-turned out as the horse itself. Men generally wear a collar and tie with a hacking jacket, tidy slacks, and a bowler hat or cap as appropriate. Women can wear the same either with a hunting cap or headscarf. Shoes should be sensible and non-slip, and suitable for running the horse up in-hand. Neat and tidy skirts are acceptable but high fashion clothes are quite inappropriate. Remember, it is the horse or pony rather than the handler who is being judged and the handler must complement rather than detract from the animal. Jeans, tee-shirts, sweat shirts and anoraks are definitely not right for in-hand showing. A show cane should always be carried and gloves worn.

Dressed for the occasion – the winner of the decorated Shire class and his handler would be the envy of many. Many handlers of native ponies and heavy horses wear plain white coats.

Clothes for the groom

The groom is very important to the show exhibitor and is responsible for keeping the animal looking its best throughout the class. Because of the chores that have to be carried out to produce the horse looking

63

good it is not always easy for the groom to keep himself or herself immaculate. However, neatness in the ring is expected and a tidy coat over a shirt and tie is not difficult to achieve. Either jodhpurs or neat tidy slacks should be worn. A riding hat finishes off the picture. The groom is a very good indication of what sort of establishment the animal comes from.

On the day

Make sure your own riding kit is complete, with boots, breeches or jodhpurs, spurs if necessary, collar, tie and/or stock and stock-pin, tweed and/or blue or black coat, gloves, whip, hunting cap, bowler or top hat as applicable, some safety pins for emergencies, and for ladies a bun, pins and hairnets as necessary. Take some spare large jeans to wear over your breeches to keep the latter clean, and take extra footwear, especially if it is likely to be wet. Remember always to take a clothes brush.

For in-hand classes, take a pair of wellingtons if the weather is likely to be wet and a spare pair of boots or suitable shoes for running in. Make sure you come prepared for the weather, with plenty of waterproof clothing at hand.

Recommended dress for ridden and working hunter classes

County shows
- Bowler hat; bowler or hunting cap for women.
- Tweed coat for men; tweed coat or plain blue or black coat for women.
- Plain fawn or buff-coloured breeches, not white.
- Plain black or brown boots.
- Garter straps – points must face outwards and the buckle should lie between buttons on breeches.
- Spurs – these must be high on heel of boot and horizontal. Judges do not wear spurs.
- Any form of string or leather glove.
- Plain Malacca or leather-covered cane.
- Collar and ordinary tie – tie must be pinned down.
- Ordinary shirt.

London and Royal shows
In the morning: as for county shows (above).
In the evening:
- Hunting dress with hunting whips. Men wear a scarlet or black hunt

coat, either ordinary pattern or cut-away. White breeches must be worn with scarlet coat, and boots with tops and white garter straps. White breeches must only be worn with top boots. Top hat should be worn.
- Women wear a black or blue hunting coat with bowler hat or hunting cap, plus fawn breeches and black boots with garter straps. Some women now wear top hats in the evening.

Side-saddle classes
County shows: ordinary habit with collar and tie and bowler hat and veil.
Royal shows: as for county shows, or habit with hunting tie; top hat and veil may be worn.
London shows: as for county shows in the morning. Habit with hunting tie; top hat and veil for the evening.

Recommended dress for hunter breeding classes
- Men should wear a suit or coat and trousers, collar and tie and a bowler hat.
- Women may wear a coat and trousers with a collar and tie or must otherwise be tidily and neatly dressed.

Ladies' hunters at the Royal Windsor Horse Show, their riders dressed in top hats and veils with hunting ties. The higher top hats, rather than the flatter Continental style, are favoured in the show ring. Bowler hats with veils and collar and tie are worn at county level and smaller shows.

Recommended dress for hack, cob and riding horse classes

County shows
- Bowler hat for men; bowler or hunting cap for women.
- Tweed coat for men; tweed coat or plain black or blue coat for women.
- Plain fawn or buff-coloured breeches, not white.
- Plain black or brown boots.
- Garter straps – points must face outwards and the buckle must lie between buttons on breeches.
- Spurs – these must be high on the heel of the boot and horizontal. Judges do not wear spurs.
- Any form of leather or string gloves.
- Plain Malacca or leather-covered cane.
- Collar and ordinary tie – tie must be pinned down.
- Ordinary shirt.

London and Royal shows
In the morning: as for county shows (above).
In the evening:

COBS
- Hunting dress with hunting whips.
- Men wear scarlet or black hunting coat, either ordinary pattern or cut-away. White breeches must be worn with scarlet coats, and boots with tops and white garter straps; white breeches with black-patent top boots may be worn with black coats, or coloured breeches and plain black boots. Top hat to be worn.
- Women wear black or blue hunting coat with bowler hat or hunting cap, plus fawn breeches and black boots with garter straps. Some women now wear top hats in the evening.

RIDING HORSES
- As for hacks (below).

HACKS
- Ladies wear top hat with white stock, plus breeches, black boots and plain or cut-away blue or black coat.
- Gentlemen wear black morning coat with tight-fitting black riding trousers with ordinary collar and tie or cravat.

SIDE-SADDLE HACKS AND RIDING HORSES
- *County shows:* Ordinary habit, black or blue with collar and tie and bowler hat and veil.
- *Royal shows* – In the morning, as for county shows. Hunting tie, top hat and veil for the evening and for finals.

A picture of supreme elegance. The champion hack with Robert Oliver in frock coat, overalls and top hat, correctly attired for the final or championship at The Horse of the Year Show.

67

A tidy line of children's ponies being given a final inspection by the judge. Children wear black or blue coats and hunting caps with jodhpurs and jodhpur boots. Elastic should be sewn on to the bottoms of jodhpurs, round the foot, to prevent them sliding up. Coloured browbands are usual for show pony classes.

Recommended dress for children's classes

- Tweed or blue/black coats in leading-rein and first ridden classes.
- Blue/black coats for show classes.
- Tweed coats for working hunter and show hunter pony classes.
- Crash hats with blue or black cover – compulsory for jumping.
- Cream or beige jodhpurs.
- Black or brown jodhpur boots.
- Plain shirt and tie.
- Girls' hair should be neatly plaited, bunched or in a hairnet if necessary.
- Handlers should be neatly dressed.
- Side-saddle classes – habit with collar and tie, gloves and hunting cap; hair neatly tied back.
- Leather or string gloves.
- Show cane.
- No spurs.

CHAPTER · 7

SHOW TACK

The tack that you show your horse in is very important as in some cases it can influence the looks of your horse. Whether ridden or in-hand the tack must complement the horse, be suitable for the type of horse, be safe and secure and, above all, be clean and well polished.

Ridden classes

The **bridle** of choice for all ridden classes is the double bridle. This is always correct in the show ring. Three- and four-year-olds, however, are encouraged to wear snaffle bridles. A pelham can be used if the horse or pony is not quite ready for the double but can cause horses to overbend. Pelhams with couplings are very useful in children's classes as little hands often find two reins a bit much to cope with. Whatever the bridle, make sure the reins are not too long. Loops of leather rein hanging down look unsightly, and children can get their feet caught up in them. The bridle should be neat and tidy with all the keepers working properly to keep all ends in place. Decorative stitching is attractive and suitable for hacks, children's show ponies and riding horses but would be considered inappropriate for hunters, cobs, working hunters and some mountain and moorlands which are unplaited. These should have good strong-looking bridles relative to their size. Plaited leather reins are acceptable and give a little more grip.

Coloured browbands are usual in hack and show pony classes. These should be neat and tidily finished at the ends and not too ostentatious. They should be the correct size for the animal concerned.

The noseband can improve or detract from the look of the animal if it has rather a long head or one that is excessively short. A wide noseband and wide browband have the effect of shortening the head. A small head is not a fault but will look better with a narrow noseband and matching browband. Very elegant animals, such as hacks and show ponies, will generally be best in narrow leather bridles, whilst the hunter and working types need sensible wider leather ones.

Saddles should be carefully considered to ensure that they suit the horse's make and shape. Show saddles are cut very straight to show

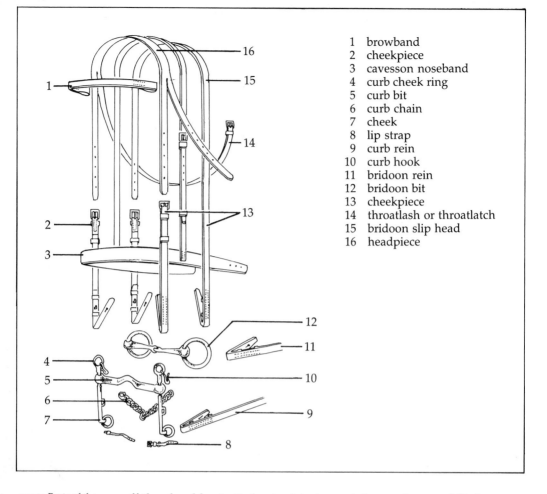

1 browband
2 cheekpiece
3 cavesson noseband
4 curb cheek ring
5 curb bit
6 curb chain
7 cheek
8 lip strap
9 curb rein
10 curb hook
11 bridoon rein
12 bridoon bit
13 cheekpiece
14 throatlash or throatlatch
15 bridoon slip head
16 headpiece

ABOVE Parts of the double bridle. Assemble as shown, with two buckles on the off side and three on the near side.

off the shoulder to its best advantage. A forward-cut saddle is apt to cover up the horse's front. On the show horse the saddle should be set back as far as possible and should be comfortable to sit on, especially if the judge is going to ride. This is most important; it is difficult enough having to assess a horse quickly without struggling with an uncomfortable saddle as well.

Girths should be either leather (used generally for hunters, cobs, riding horses and working hunters) or well-whitened webbing (more usual for ponies and hacks). The width of the girth and size of the saddle can enhance or detract from your horse especially if it tends to be on the long side. A little saddle with narrow girths will look fine on a short-coupled animal but may look ridiculous on a slightly longer-backed horse, so with this type use a larger saddle and broad girths placed a little further back to 'shorten' the horse.

OPPOSITE ABOVE This line-up of four-year-old hunters shows some in snaffle bridles. These are encouraged for this age, as they are for children's ponies.

Remember to be sure that the **irons** and **leathers** will be the right size for the judge. If yours are too small or too large have your groom bring in an appropriately sized pair for the judge to use. There is nothing

LEFT For working hunters and working ponies plain bridles with any type of bit are allowed, plus martingales, but this must not be changed for the showing phase. Katie Adam on Towy Valley Maurice are well dressed for the parade at the Royal.

RIGHT A typical straight-cut show saddle, which shows off the horse's front and shoulder to its best advantage. Numnahs, if used, should be as discreet as possible. Be sure the stirrups used will fit the judge and that leathers can be shortened or lengthened to suit.

more frustrating than having to ride a strange horse when you can hardly get your feet into the irons, or to find the leathers do not have enough holes in to either shorten or lengthen them for comfort. At that moment it would not be surprising if the judge awarded you at least one black mark, and will probably be less sympathetic if your horse makes even a minor mistake. Look ahead and think what is required. In an emergency another competitor may have a suitable pair you can borrow, but it is always best to be self-sufficient. It can be a little embarrassing if you subsequently beat the kind person who lent you his or her equipment!

Try your horse in a few different bridles and saddles and take a critical look at him so that you can see for yourself what he looks like and which seems right for his make and shape.

Numnahs are not really correct for the show horse and should not be necessary with a good well-fitting saddle, but if you must use one ensure it is very discreet. Pure wool ones can be cut to the exact shape of your saddle. White numnahs look fine on greys, but a black or brown one may look better with a darker animal. If used, numnahs must be spotlessly clean, especially the white ones, if they are not to seriously detract from the overall picture.

For leading-rein classes, a neat **lead rein** of leather or whitened webbing is required. It should be attached to the noseband only.

For **side-saddle** classes, the saddle must fit correctly, sitting evenly and squarely either side of the back bone. It is important that it is regularly checked over to ensure it is in good condition and that it is the right shape for your horse as any unevenness will detract from your performance. The stirrup must be adjustable and should allow the hand to fit in between your leg and the leaping head when mounted. This ensures there is enough room to raise your heel up into the leaping head for extra security when necessary. The girth should be the correct length for your horse – this is worth checking carefully each year. There is nothing worse than discovering at the beginning of the season that the girth is just too short or too long and unsafe for riding. Some saddles have the girth and balance strap combined, which is easier to cope with in the show ring, but they must be the right length. The type that has a separate balance strap must be carefully checked to ensure that the strap does not get left behind. It is a wise precaution to leave one end attached to the saddle at all times.

In-hand classes

To show in-hand the horse requires a neat show bridle or headcollar, depending on its age and class, with the correct turnout being mentioned in the relevant charts at the back of the book.

Most youngstock are shown in a plain in-hand bridle with a rubber bit and a lead rein. Some stallion bridles have discreet metalwork, but fillies are normally shown in a plain bridle. Broodmares are often led in a double bridle although some mountain and moorland breeds are led in a well-polished headcollar and rope or in a halter. Some heavy horses are led in a white rope or webbing halter. Foals are always led in a foal slip and should never have a bit in their mouths. Yearlings may need a rubber bit but two- and three-year-olds should have preferably a rubber or round, soft bit in their mouths and must be handled sympathetically as it is at this time that many young mouths are ruined.

Whatever bridle is used it must fit properly and improve the look of the animal. The bits, buckles or brasswork should be beautifully polished and if a white halter or lead rope is used this must be well whitened.

Some stallions are best shown in a show roller with side reins to ensure they stay straight and show themselves off. This may or may not require a crupper to prevent it sliding forward. All should be very well polished and of a neat plain design so that it enhances the appearance of the animal. Some Arabs are now shown in lightweight Arab-style bridles. Unfortunately these are often not strong enough and several horses have got loose. It is most important to check that all tack used is sufficiently strong as loose horses at a show are a frightening sight for humans and equines alike and several unnecessary accidents have been caused in this way.

Many different breed societies have their own set of rules and although the charts at the back of this book give a good guide, always check carefully through your rule books and show schedules to be certain that there are no specific guidelines mentioned as to how the animal should appear before the judge.

On the day

When going through your tack for the show be sure you have the essentials: saddle, bridle, girth, irons and leathers and show cane, plus a spare clean girth in case the weather is bad and one gets filthy during your exercising period. Better still, take a spare set of tack with you for use when exercising, then your show set is ready, clean and polished, for the class. Some animals are best lunged before their class, so the lungeing kit of cavesson, lunge rein, roller, side reins, bridle and lunge whip, plus a set of protective boots, should also be taken. Boots or bandages are a wise precaution at shows, as it is on just such occasions that the animal has a fright or is feeling a bit fresh and knocks or strikes into itself. Putting these on, at least until it has settled down and

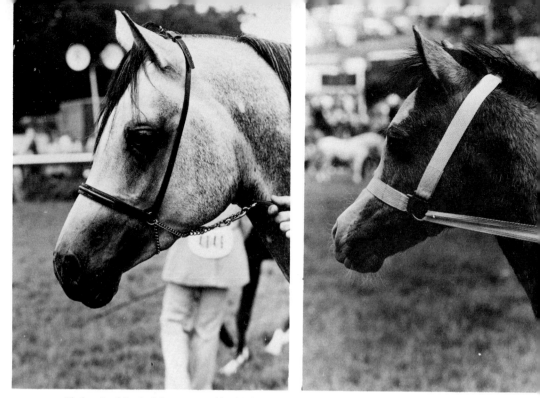

ABOVE LEFT *The beauty of the Arab is accentuated by this fine show halter; slender exotic bridles are sometimes used for the pure-bred classes. Be sure that the tack is strong enough to control the animal – safety must come first and foremost.*

ABOVE RIGHT *A nice broad halter is ideal for leading foals. There are numerous different types but wide ones such as this will be less likely to rub.*

BELOW LEFT *A neat in-hand show bridle with brass browband, loose-ringed bit and leather lead rein, suitable for pony youngstock.*

BELOW RIGHT *A plain, fine leather show halter with a leather coupling. Plain show bridles or halters are considered best for coloured, spotted or unusual breeds and are always correct. If in doubt about show bridles, use a fairly plain one that shows your horse off to its best advantage. The judge wants to look at the animal, not at what it is wearing.*

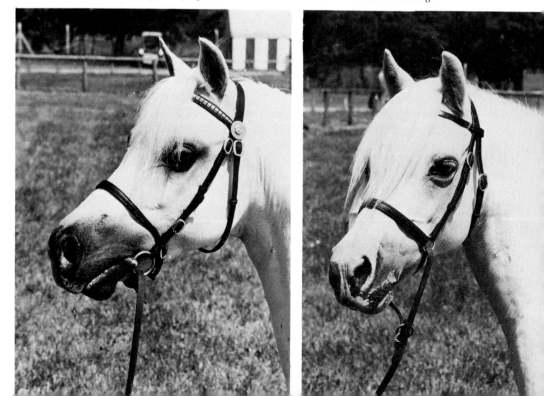

always when lungeing, is sensible. The in-hand animal will require its in-hand bridle, and show roller and side reins if used. A spare lead rein is worth having just in case anything goes wrong, as are a spare headcollar and lead rope.

Hay and water plus a feed is essential to keep the animal happy and contented; it will help to settle a youngster if he has something to nibble at during the day. Don't forget buckets and feed bins.

The grooming kit, with all necessary brushes, oils and plaiting equipment, plus a clean brush, sponge and stable rubber to take into the ring, should be included.

Rugs, sheets and waterproofs should be packed to cater for unpredictable weather, plus a smart well-fitting roller or surcingle.

Travelling kit, including knee caps and hock boots if necessary, should be worn for the journey. The tail needs to be well protected with a bandage and tail guard. Loosely plaiting the tail and folding it up, or putting on a nylon stocking to keep it clean, will save one more chore on arrival at the show.

If your horse is not a good traveller extra protection may be necessary to prevent it damaging itself. Bandaging the legs then putting on travel boots which incorporate knee and hock protection, may help. A poll guard to protect the head is also wise. Allow the horse as much space in the box as possible and drive very slowly, especially if the roads are twisty. Give yourself extra time for travelling with a difficult horse as so much depends on gaining his confidence, something which can never be done if you are in a hurry. Make sure the floor is not slippery.

Always have your tack-cleaning kit with you, and take boot polish for your own boots and any tack that needs buffing up. Metal polish and a duster are also a must.

To beat the weather Vin Toulson has donned mac and bowler hat and looks just as immaculate leading his hunter breeding champion as he does when riding. Note the sensible, plain strong bridle and coupling used for the hunter.

75

CHAPTER 8

PRESENTATION

Producing the horse for the ring is an art that takes years to perfect. The plaiting, turn-out, grooming, way of going and general condition of the horse or pony combine to make the overall picture that you present to the judge. Naturally you will want to attract his attention early on in the class, especially when the ring is teeming with other exhibits.

Manes and tails

Plaiting can make an enormous difference to your horse's appearance. A poor neck can be improved tremendously by pulling the plaits upwards on to the top of the neck and then rolling them up so they rest neatly and evenly on top. If the plaits are pulled down on this type of neck they accentuate the problem. A poor neck will not improve your showing prospects, so unless you can plait it cosmetically to improve the outline your chances of success will be not great until the neck improves.

A horse with an overdeveloped crest will need its neckline fined down. The mane should therefore be well pulled, and small plaits should be rolled down on to the neck to ensure no extra prominence is given.

A good neck should be enhanced by beautifully neat and even plaits all the way down the neck. Remember no plaits will look really good unless the mane has been well pulled and is all the same length before you start.

Before you set about pulling a mane be quite sure that you do not intend to show your horse or pony in classes for mountain and moorlands, palominos, pure-bred Arabs, etc., as in many of these classes manes should be left natural, although some discreet tidying is usually permitted. If you need to plait these animals for other classes it is best to have a couple of practice sessions at home to see which size plait produces the best result.

Elastic bands, by the way, should never be used for showing; all plaits must be sewn in place with thread or wool of a suitable colour.

Heavy horses are normally plaited or braided with raffia or coloured

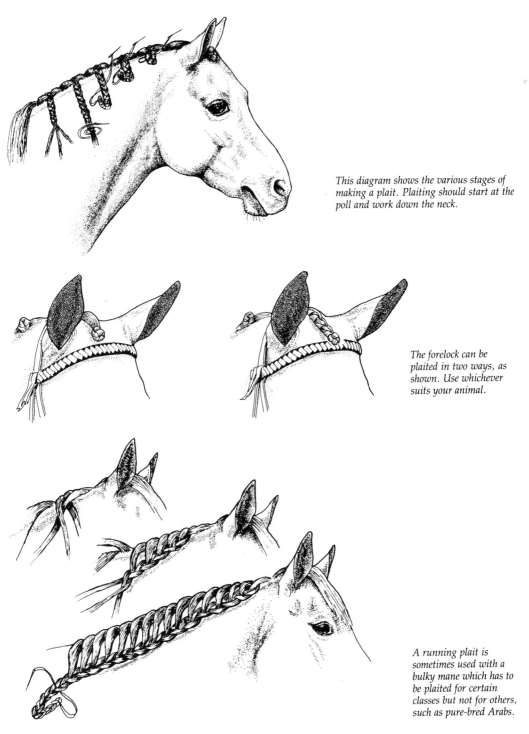

This diagram shows the various stages of making a plait. Plaiting should start at the poll and work down the neck.

The forelock can be plaited in two ways, as shown. Use whichever suits your animal.

A running plait is sometimes used with a bulky mane which has to be plaited for certain classes but not for others, such as pure-bred Arabs.

This method of tail plaiting produces a flat central plait. Tightness is essential for a neat result.

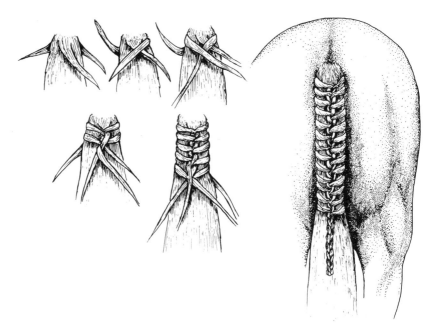

This method of plaiting produces a raised central plait. Always take in even-sized strands of hair and finish off neatly.

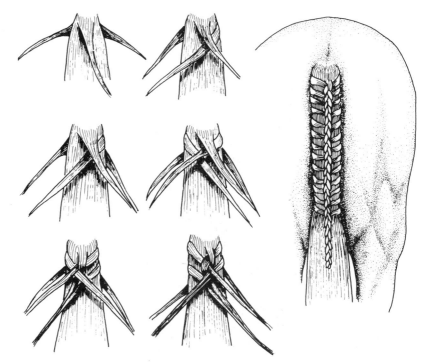

wool, and plenty of practice is required to perfect the technique. Their tails are also put up or the docks clipped.

Tail plaiting should enhance the shape of the quarters and the look of the tail. To be successful the tail hairs at the top need to be quite long, preferably never having been pulled, and the plaiting should continue down the tail just far enough to give a good line to the quarters.

The tail plait should be neatly finished off, usually by being looped back on itself and stitched in place. Once plaited, make sure you curve the tail nicely into the shape of the quarters so that the end hangs naturally.

If the tail is pulled this should be neat and tidy and kept well bandaged during the day so that it remains in shape. The increasing practice of using razors and clippers on tails is a very sad reflection of the times. Once this has been done it becomes extremely difficult to pull a tail properly afterwards. The razor ruins the looks of the tail, leaving almost bald sides which must be extremely prickly as they start to grow again – it is hardly surprising that one sees so many show horses going round the ring with tails clamped in.

Once a properly pulled tail is as you require it, and it may well take a

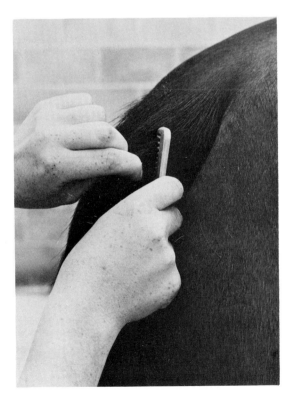

Tail pulling: start at the sides, then pull evenly downwards and a little from the middle. Don't overdo the pulling so that bald patches appear; and don't be tempted to clip the sides.

week or so to get it that way with the more sensitive horses, it only requires a few minutes a week to keep it looking good.

The length is important and for most ridden animals 4 ins (10 cm) below the point of hock is a good rough guide. Before cutting the tail, however, always study how your horse carries its tail. Some carry them high, others low, and it is this, and what will look best for your particular horse, that will be the deciding factors.

When you cut the tail place your arm under the dock to raise it into the horse's normal carrying position, then ask an assistant to cut it straight across at the required length.

Too long a tail can detract from the overall balance of the show horse. In Britain the 'bang' tail has been in vogue for years but in other countries a longer tail is more usual.

As stated earlier, be sure never to brush out the bottom of the tail as this causes hairs to be pulled out.

Trimming

Trimming of the show horse is another important aspect but with many pure-bred mountain and moorland classes, heavy horses, etc., feather is left natural so, don't get carried away until you are quite sure that you have decided which classes you wish to enter.

Use clippers or scissors to trim the head, jaw, whiskers and ears. All trimming should be done discreetly, making it look as natural as possible. This is generally quite easy with the finer breeds, which tend not to carry excess hair. Ears are usually tidied up down the front and trimmed slightly inside if they tend to be too fluffy.

A small section of mane just behind the ears should be removed to allow the bridle or headcollar to 'sit' comfortably. When clipping or timming this area take care not to remove too wide a section – about 1–1½ ins (25–35 mm) is about right. The practice of cutting the mane right back at the poll and doing the same at the withers ruins the look of the horse and is definitely not to be encouraged.

Whiskers are generally clipped or trimmed off the lighter types of animal, such as ponies, hacks and riding horses, but may be left on hunters, cobs, native breeds, heavy horses, etc., although very long whiskers may need a slight tidy up.

The heels are usually trimmed for all ridden show classes and can either be done with clippers or a comb and scissors. Care must be taken not to create a 'stepped' look, so trimming must be neat and even.

Heavy breeds and mountain and moorlands with feathers etc. are usually left natural but produced spotlessly clean and well brushed. White feather is often whitened with chalk to enhance the colour and then well brushed on the day of the show.

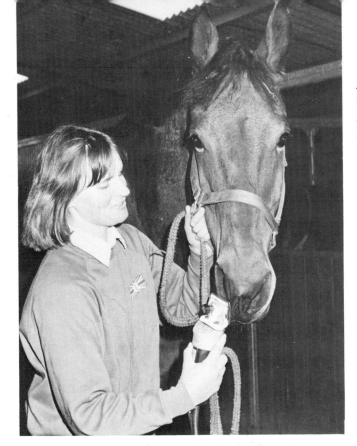

Most show horses have their whiskers trimmed but some people prefer to leave them natural on hunters and cobs. The whiskers of native ponies and the heavy-horse breeds are usually left untrimmed.

BELOW Polo ponies are not often shown except ridden, dressed for a match. This pony has just come in from its winter rest and is about to be hogged and prepared for its new season.

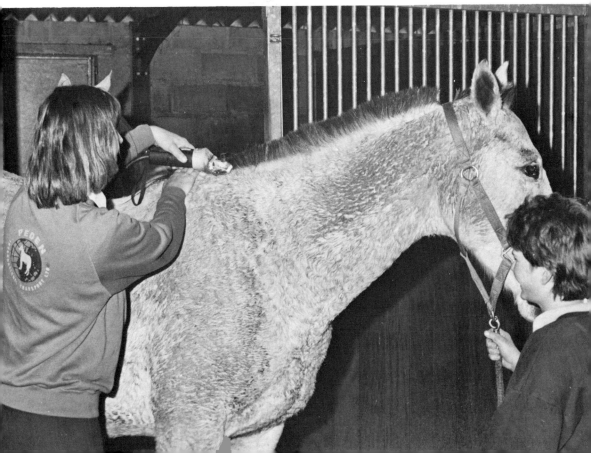

Washing

Washing of the horse is often carried out a few days before a show, or the day before if the horse is liable to sweat. It is seldom necessary to do this with all types but the mane and tail should be washed before a show; also the legs from knees and hocks downwards. Be careful not to give your horse a chill if washing him all over. Wash the mane and body quickly then rug him up well before finishing off the tail and legs. A brisk walk afterwards will warm him up and ensure he does not get cold.

If the horse has been well groomed daily, a wash is usually only indicated if he actually looks dirty, but many people wash automatically before a show, especially in hot weather. Use a good brand of horse shampoo to produce a nice shine, and avoid washing too frequently as shampoo tends to remove the natural oils in the skin and can make the coat a little fluffy, especially near coat changing time.

The coat and clipping

Rugging of the show horse is very important if its summer coat is to stay looking good throughout the season, so keeping it warm is the very first priority. This is especially necessary if you are aiming for a big show at the end of the season, such as the Horse of the Year Show which, being in October, means that most horses are just about to or have already started to get their winter coat and lose their summer bloom. Keeping the show horse warm will help to encourage the summer coat to come through early and prevent the winter one arriving too soon.

When to clip, if this is likely to be necessary, such as with ridden horses, is a difficult decision to make. It is most important that this is done before the summer coat starts to come through otherwise the clipping can damage the new growth. The show horse is best clipped right out so that no lines are left. A good clip should not leave any marks on the coat and should follow the direction of the coat throughout.

If you have to clip just before a show, providing you are good at the job, do it 24–48 hours beforehand. The clipped coat will usually look its best at this time. Do not rush into clipping the show horse, however, as it does have the effect of rather deadening the colour and few horses look as good as with their proper coat. Many beautiful bright bays turn a disappointing mouse colour on being clipped and rich chestnuts can turn into rather anaemic-looking specimens – so if you can avoid clipping, do so. Dark browns and greys are probably the two colours which are least affected.

Clipping must be carried out with a newly sharpened set of blades to ensure a smooth result. Use long, slow, sweeping strokes against the lie of the coat.

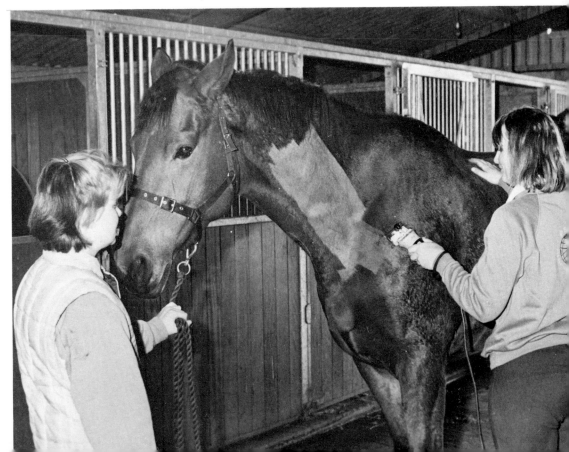

Make sure you have a new or newly sharpened set of blades on your clippers before starting. This is essential to produce a professional finish. Keep the horse well covered and warm afterwards. In the autumn some people keep hoods on their horses to encourage the coat to stay flat and grow at the same rate. Use of an infra-red light in the stable may help to keep a summer coat and encourage it to come through quicker at the beginning of the year.

Once your horse is clipped out make quite sure it has plenty of bedding – it will have lost one layer of natural protection so may need more cushioning to prevent it from scraping hocks and joints. This will also give extra warmth.

The feet

Care of the feet has already been discussed but make quite sure that your show horse's feet are in their best possible state before leaving for the show. The feet of youngstock and other animals without shoes may require a quick rasp on the day you travel to ensure there are no rough edges. Some exhibitors polish the feet with boot polish before a show, which has the advantage of being less messy than hoof oil. Either method is excellent. Some people clean white stripes on hooves by rubbing lightly with sandpaper. For best effect, the feet should be attended to just before entering the ring.

Finishing touches

The final touches before going into the ring include darkening the eye lids and nostrils with a little oil or Vaseline to accentuate the quality of the head. These areas and the dock should be sponged first and then wiped over with a very small amount of oil without making the area sticky. Cosmetic black eye shadow can also be used.

Hairspray can be helpful in controlling a difficult mane that refuses to plait well; and can be usefully kept with the show grooming kit for emergencies.

Diamonds and shark's teeth markings on the quarters are often used to add a little extra elegance to the hack, child's show pony and riding horse. They are sometimes seen on hunters and may also be used in some part-bred classes.

If applied they should be neat and add to the overall outlook of the animal; in no way should they detract from it or draw the eye away from the animal as a whole.

Diamonds can be put on with a small comb broken to about 1–1½ ins (25–35 mm) long, and with the coat brushed smoothly on the quarters, drawing it downwards in a type of chequer-board design. Alter-

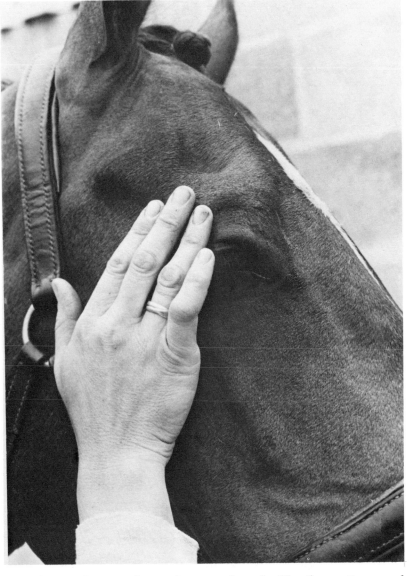

natively templates can be made or purchased with other patterns and shapes. These are placed on the quarters and held still while the underlying hair is brushed downwards to leave the imprint. Some people use templates whose patterns are too large for their animal, which spoils the effect, so be careful to choose one that is right for your horse or pony or, better still, put on your own pattern.

Shark's teeth can add interest and need practice. They should be started a little below the hip bone and put on in long sweeping strokes,

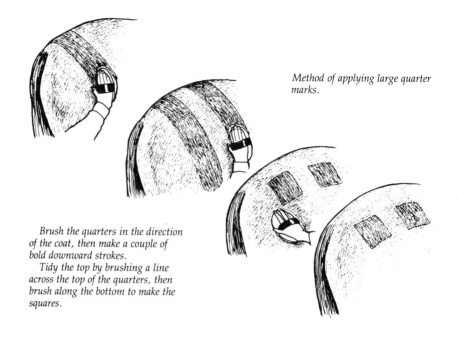

Method of applying large quarter marks.

Brush the quarters in the direction of the coat, then make a couple of bold downward strokes.

Tidy the top by brushing a line across the top of the quarters, then brush along the bottom to make the squares.

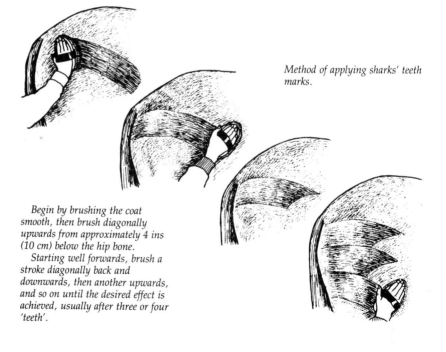

Method of applying sharks' teeth marks.

Begin by brushing the coat smooth, then brush diagonally upwards from approximately 4 ins (10 cm) below the hip bone.

Starting well forwards, brush a stroke diagonally back and downwards, then another upwards, and so on until the desired effect is achieved, usually after three or four 'teeth'.

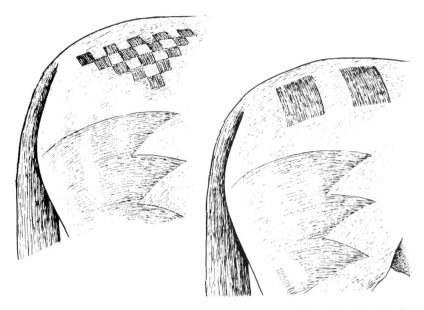

Two different designs for quarter marks. For some animals a better effect will be achieved by first damping the coat well with a sponge; however, do not overdo this or the marks will look untidy as the coat dries.

making one upward stroke then one downward one, leaving a neat line of 'teeth' down the quarters. Unless these are done well they do not look good so do practise frequently at home before attempting to do them for the show ring.

It hardly needs to be stated that if your horse's back end is not its strong point then for goodness sake don't draw attention to it, especially with shark's teeth. These will show off your horse's inadequacies more obviously if the quarters are rather weak and lacking roundness.

Once you feel you have your horse more or less ready for the ring, stand back to admire your handiwork and to ensure that the overall picture is right. The tack should look clean and sparkling, the coat should be gleaming following a final dust over. Diamonds and shark's teeth, if used, should have been well applied. The tail should have been well separated by hand or *lightly* brushed out with a soft brush; the hooves should be oiled. The plaits should have been checked, any untidy hairs sorted out and the tail bandage removed. If the mane is unplaited this should have been thoroughly brushed out, including the forelock. The handler (if appropriate) should be ready, looking equally neat and tidy, wearing the appropriate number and, if necessary, carrying any certificates relevant to the class.

87

Foxton Flight heads an attractive line-up of hacks, all beautifully plaited and presented, in elegant bridles with coloured browbands and comfortable straight-cut saddles. It is, however, correct to wear spurs with long boots. If necessary, the dummy sort can be worn.

For ridden classes check the saddle is in the right place, not too far forward, so that the horse is shown off to its best advantage. The rider should be neat, clean and tidy with coat well brushed and boots highly polished. Gloves, spurs and a show cane, plus the correct number, must be worn and any relevant certificates carried in the pocket.

Be prepared

Make quite sure you know where the rings are, which one you are in, and the number of your class. Arrive at the collecting ring at least five minutes before the scheduled starting time of your class. Many youngstock classes start at a set time with each class following on afterwards, so keep a constant check to ensure you don't miss yours as some of these are judged very quickly. Listen carefully for any announcements regarding your class and the day's schedule as changes do sometimes take place.

Careful planning of the day needs to be worked out before you set off and this will very much depend on the distance to be travelled, but the most essential aspect of showing is to allow yourself plenty of time to be able to prepare your horse looking and behaving at its best.

Most showgrounds become notoriously short of space once all the horseboxes have arrived and the car parks begin to fill up so it is worth arriving early if you want to exercise. Ridden horses must be well mannered and the young ones in particular may require quite some time to settle down. The older horse sometimes tends to get a little ring crafty, so again may need ample work to ensure it is going at its best. Children's ponies often require riding or lungeing well before the child gets on, so a suitable spot should be found for lungeing if necessary. Youngsters may need a little exercise before entering the ring and if possible a quiet area should be found to trot them around in, but usually these animals tend to tire quite quickly once the initial excitement wears off. Three-year-olds, however, may need a little serious work before entering the ring if they are the exuberant type.

The best way to ensure the animals are fairly well behaved is to give them plenty of work the day before so that they are less likely to sweat and get in a lather on the day of the show. Quiet walking after an initial trot and canter round is often the best way as it relaxes the horse and gives it a chance to settle into its surroundings. If this does not seem to be working, for goodness sake get on and work it as behaviour is much more important than looks. A badly behaved animal is unlikely to do well and will quickly earn a bad reputation. The sooner you can sort it out with plenty of work, the better.

Many is the time I've had to ride a show horse right up to fifteen minutes before a class because it was being so silly. I've then quickly washed it down, kept it walking to dry it off, gone into the ring and won; meanwhile others have been fussing over their horse's coat, mindless of whether their horse was going sensibly enough to enter the ring. With showing it is most important to get your priorities right.

It is sad to see so many good horses being produced so badly – it makes one weep. I have often seen horses much better looking than my own, sitting at the bottom of the line because the owner did not know or was incapable of learning from others what was required for a particular class.

However well made your horse or pony, if it is not produced in the ring according to the accepted way for that class, you are unlikely to be noticed. It is no good moaning that the judge is no good; instead, you must set about looking and learning what is required and ensure that by the next outing you and your show horse are produced properly. If you want to show seriously, study the form at the top shows; make sure you have a good picture of what is required. You will seldom see the best animals at the smaller ones, so you have to think big if you want to acquire the right ideas.

To look and be professional be quite sure you know what is expected of you for each class and be prepared for it. Try to be in the right place to catch the judge's eye when your chance comes. Watch the judge discreetly to be sure you are ready when he asks for a change of pace. Avoid doing this in front of him unless you are sure your horse will look good at that moment. It is usually best to remain in trot or canter until you have passed the judge. When called into a small circle for the final line-up, put yourself in a good position and don't allow yourself to be obscured by other riders. A judge will not pull you in if he can't see you so make sure that you are always in the best position with your animal looking and going its best at all times – this is really what presentation is all about.

Recommendations for turn-out

Ridden and working hunters
- Manes should be plaited.
- Tails pulled or plaited.
- Heels trimmed.
- Double bridle or pelham; four-year olds are encouraged to be shown in a snaffle.
- Martingales are only to be used on working hunters.
- Browbands must be plain.
- Saddles should be reasonably straight cut.
- Ordinary shoes.

Hunter breeding classes
- Manes should be plaited; there is no need to plait foals.
- Tails pulled or plaited; foals may be plaited or natural.
- Heels trimmed; there is no need to trim foals' heels.
- Led hunters should be shown in leather headcollars or bridles; two- and three-year-olds should have bits. Yearlings may have bits but foals should wear just a leather headslip.

Hacks and riding horses
- Manes should be plaited.
- Tails pulled.
- Heels trimmed.
- Double bridle or pelham.
- Saddles should be reasonably straight cut.
- Shoes of light steel or aluminium plate.
- Coloured browbands.
- Numnahs, if worn, should be as discreet as possible.

Cobs
- Manes should be hogged.
- Tails pulled and cut short in length.
- Strong double bridle or pelham.
- Saddle should be reasonably straight cut.
- Browbands must be plain.
- Ordinary shoes of light steel or aluminium plate.

Children's ponies
- Manes plaited.
- Tails pulled or plaited.
- Neatly trimmed.
- Snaffle bridle for leading rein and four-year-olds.
- Double or pelham.
- Light shoes if used.
- Coloured browbands.
- Plain browbands for show hunter ponies.
- Working hunter ponies – as above but optional tack with plain browband. Martingales are allowed.

Side-saddle classes
- Double bridle or pelham.
- Plain browbands for hunters and cobs.
- Coloured browbands for hacks, riding horses and ponies.
- Manes plaited.
- Tails pulled or plaited.

Additional information on turn-out can be found in the reference charts at the back of the book.

91

CHAPTER 9

TIPS FOR EXHIBITORS

There are certain crucial points relating to exhibiting which can make all the difference to the enjoyment of a day's showing:

1. Allow plenty of time for the journey and for preparing your animal for the ring.

2. Come well prepared for all eventualities, especially the weather; take spares in case of breakages; and plenty of food for equines and humans in case of long waits.

3. Be a good sport. Only one animal can win the class and crabbing the winner, if it isn't yourself, is not going to change the result. The judge has to weigh all the pros and cons and is the only person who can see all of these. Everyone has his or her preference for a certain type, but it is the judge on the day who decides.

4. Never be rude or abusive to judges, stewards or officials. Not only is such behaviour appalling, but you could well end up being refused further entries, or worse. By all means quietly ask the judge after the class why he or she didn't like your horse, and if he feels there is anything you could do to improve it or its way of going. This is the way to learn and get the most out of showing.

5. Never be late for your class. If you are, always go straight up to the judge or steward, apologise and ask if it is acceptable for you to join in. In some cases it may be, but if judging has already commenced you may have to retire gracefully, despite a 4 am start or a 50-mile journey. It is *your* responsibility to be there on time.

6. Make quite sure you know your rules. It is embarrassing for everyone to see people doing things which are incorrect, whether done in ignorance or not, and the offending exhibitor simply looks stupid. Read the rules carefully each year, especially any new ones. All rules have been brought in for a reason and the onus is on you to know them and stick by them.

A smile that sums up a successful day, making all the effort seem worthwhile, from Lucy Boyatt and Wharf Evangeline.

Three outstanding professionals of the show ring, Robert Oliver, Vin Toulson and Peter Richmond weighing up the opposition in the hunter class at the Three Counties Show. Note the well-polished strong bridle used for the hunter and the correct angle of the bowler hats, worn horizontal to the ground.

7. Support your breed society or show association in every way you can to increase interest and enjoyment of that particular type of horse and class. If it is a new society or needs extra classes put on, lobby your local shows to include these in their schedules. If you can help by producing a sponsor they will usually be happy to consider it, but make quite sure you get plenty of support for any extra classes they include.

8. Above all, enjoy your day. If things go well, you will do this anyway, but that cannot happen always, so make the best of your day and look forward to the next outing, which may be more lucky for you. It would be an extremely dull world if everyone liked the same things, and while your horse may be a star to some, others will prefer a different type; you will have to wait for success under another judge. Very often things go so badly wrong you can only laugh; but whatever happens, so long as you and your horse or pony have enjoyed yourselves it will always be worth doing. When the fun aspect no longer exists you may just as well give up because you will never be satisfied.

CHAPTER · 10

TIPS FOR JUDGES

Judging can be an enjoyable and rewarding activity and there is always a shortage of new judges coming forward. It is hoped that would-be judges will find the following tips helpful:

1. Never arrive late for your class. To do so will cause absolute chaos; in addition, your reputation will be shattered as no one will ever rely on you again. The onus is on you to arrive and present yourself, ready to judge, at the secretary's office or designated spot at least fifteen minutes before your class is scheduled; if the show is running behind schedule, make sure the secretary knows where to find you while you wait.

2. Be consistent throughout the day. Don't put animals down for misbehaving in one class and ignore the same sort of antics in the next; and if possible stick to type.

3. Avoid obviously noticing conformational faults and blemishes. A good judge should spot curbs etc. without having to feel down the back of the hock. Some competitors love to crab and will relish the opportunity of criticising another's horse if they have seen you looking at a part of it with suspicion, whether or not it has a problem. If you must look or feel legs, do it to *all* the exhibits rather than pick out one or two for special scrutiny.

4. If you can't tell a horse's age (which all judges should be able to do) ask the competitor, but don't go into its breeding or other details during the class. This is particularly important with breeding classes and will quickly get you a bad name if you enquire before the classes are finished.

5. Never look at a catalogue before your class is completed. The judge should come to the class fresh, with no pre-knowledge of who or what will appear before him. Anyone seen studying details of the entries beforehand lays himself open to all sorts of criticism. It is, however, considered normal for the organisers to give you a free catalogue on completion of the judging, and it is interesting to read it afterward. Your steward should arrange this for you.

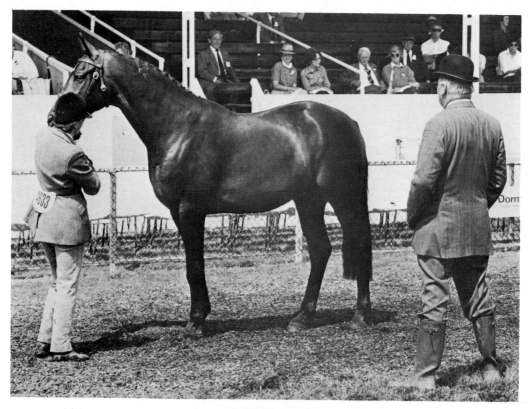

ABOVE *Assessing each horse is a difficult job but every exhibitor deserves a fair deal. If you are judging a huge class, have your steward make simple notes of anything you particularly want to remember.*

RIGHT *All judges are expected to be neatly dressed and many societies stipulate hats for ladies. It is usually best to wear something that won't show the dirt too much, and to choose comfortable shoes as you are likely to be on your feet for some time.*

6. Check before you start judging that your steward understands how the class is to be judged and is fully conversant with the rules for judging that particular class. If he isn't, brief him carefully, and tactfully mention to the chief steward that an experienced steward for each type of class makes everything run that much smoother for everyone, and might be more appropriate for another year.

7. Inevitably there are times when you will find yourself judging those you know quite well. Never be seen talking to friends, exhibitors, or riders before the class – this will inevitably lead to gossip. Be absolutely fair and treat everyone exactly the same in the ring.

8. Don't be influenced by seeing the big names leading or riding. It is the horse that you are judging and because it is produced by a 'pro' doesn't mean it is necessarily the best in the class. The difficulty often arises, however, when the professional makes a less good horse seem better than it really is through clever presentation, which is really what showing is all about. It is not necessarily what you have got but how you present it that makes the difference between winning and losing.

If judging ridden classes the judge should wear a tweed coat and should always carry a cane; spurs should not be worn. Be fair and consistent and remember that it is the horse and not the rider who you are judging, in that class, on that day. Don't be influenced by previous form, good or bad.

9. Above all, don't be influenced by the opinions of others. You are there to judge the class and produce a line-up which *you* feel is right – unless there are two of you judging, it must be your decision on that day. Don't penalise a horse because, for example, it behaved badly last month or appeared weak behind last year. It is the horse in front of you, on that day, in that class, that you are judging.

10. Try to stick to the timetable and judge the class as quickly as possible. If there are a lot of entries and you have a limited amount of time, work out how best to organise your judging and give everyone a good chance to be seen. This may mean seeing two shows at once or, if there are two judges, sharing the riding of the second half of the line-up. Ask your steward to ensure that the horses are ready to be run up in-hand immediately when required. Children can be terribly slow about this but a good steward can soon get them organised. If you can keep up to time you will always be popular, but once you acquire a reputation for being slow, shows will be reluctant to ask you to judge.

11. Always be neat and tidy. Judges never wear spurs if riding but should carry a show cane. Ladies should wear hats in most cases for all pony and in-hand classes, so always have one with you. Go prepared for the weather.

12. Be pleasant to all, positive, fair in your decisions, and never lay yourself open to criticism. In this way you will enjoy many pleasant years of judging.

PART 2

Guidelines and Reference Charts for Individual Classes

HUNTERS

The show hunter is expected to be good-looking, workmanlike, a good galloper, well mannered and up to the right weight for its class. It must gallop well and be a pleasant ride for the judge. In working hunter classes a fluent clear round is expected, with a short, sharp gallop at the end of the round giving a good impression. The hunter should be shown in strong but plain tack. In four-year-old classes snaffle bridles are encouraged; this class is intended purely for those young horses who do not participate in the championships.

The ladies' hunter should be a good hunter type but suitable for a woman to hold and control side-saddle. It must be a comfortable ride.

The three main ridden classes are for lightweight, middleweight and heavyweight hunters. There are various classes for four-year-olds, novices, juveniles and young horses, and the suitability of the horse for the age group will have some bearing on the result. In small hunter classes the height limit is 15.2 hh and in affiliated classes a height certificate will be required for this.

At affiliated shows exhibitors must be members of the National Light Horse Breeding Society (HIS) and all ridden horses registered with the appropriate section.

An impressive line-up of lightweight hunters, headed by Jane Crofts and Periglen. Horses and riders are impeccably turned out and receiving their rosettes from judge Henrietta Knight.

HUNTERS

Ridden	Galloped	Show	Ridden by judge	Browband	Tack
Weights	√	×	√	plain	double bridle or pelham
Small	√	×	√	plain	double bridle or pelham
Novice	√	×	√	plain	as above or for 4-y-o
4-year-olds	√	×	√	plain	snaffle
Working hunters	√	×	√	plain	any

In-hand					
Broodmares	n/a	in-hand	n/a	plain	leather headcollar or double bridle
Foals	n/a	in-hand	n/a	n/a	leather foal slip
Youngstock	n/a	in-hand	n/a	plain	leather headcollar or bridle

Hunters continued

Ridden	Jumping	Height certificate	Plaiting	Martingale	Stripped	NOTES
Weights	×	×	√	×	√	
Small	×	√	√	×	√	
Novice	×	×	√	×	√	
4-year-olds	×	×	√	×	√	
Working hunters	√	×	√	optional	usually	jumping takes place but only the best rounds come forward for further judging

In-hand						
Broodmares	n/a	×	√	n/a	n/a	
Foals	n/a	×	optional	n/a	n/a	
Youngstock	n/a	×	√	n/a	n/a	yearlings may require very mild bits; 2-y-o and 3-y-o should have bits

ABOVE *Lorraine Tatlow on The Artful Dodger, winner of the ladies' hunter class at the Royal International Horse Show in Birmingham, 1988.*

BELOW *In-hand hunter classes are very popular today with youngstock classes being among the most interesting. It is hoped that exhibitors will not overfeed their youngsters for the show ring. If young horses are allowed to mature more naturally they will not become coarse or develop other problems associated with being 'overdone' as youngsters.*

ABOVE *Broodmares should be shown plaited and in double bridles. Their foals can be plaited if desired, but often look best left natural. Handling and leading from an early age will result in well-behaved and confident foals – the one shown is quite happy to walk in front of its mother.*

BELOW *Working hunters should jump fluently, at a good hunting pace, round a course of rustic jumps. The best rounds go forward for further judging.*

HACKS

The show hack should present a picture of supreme elegance. Its manners and way of going must be exemplary and it must be a pleasing, comfortable ride. A show is normally expected; it should be short but including walk, trot and canter on both reins. The hack is expected to canter on but not to gallop. If possible it should halt and rein back, or at least show a good halt, and stand still on a loose rein.

There are two height classes – exceeding 14.2 hh but not exceeding 15 hh; and exceeding 15 hh but not exceeding 15.3 hh – as well as novice, ladies and occasionally pairs.

There are now various breeding classes being held for show hacks and potential hacks and youngstock. Again elegance is the essence and these exhibits should be shown in neat show bridles with plaited manes and tails. Ridden hacks usually have pulled tails.

At affiliated shows all hacks must be registered for the current year in the appropriate section and riders and exhibitors must be members of the British Show Hack, Cob and Riding Horse Association.

HACKS

Ridden classes	Show	Ridden by judge	Galloped	Coloured browband	Height certificate	Side-saddle	Manes plaited	Double bridle or pelham
Small exc. 14.2–not exc. 15.00 *Large* exc. 15.00–not exc. 15.3	√	√	a good stride out rather than galloped	√	√	unusual	√	√
Novice exc. 14.2–not exc. 15.3	√	√	as above	√	√	as above	√	√
Ladies	√	√	as above	√	√	√	√	√
Championships	√	rarely	as above	√	√	rarely	√	√
Pairs	√	×	as above	√	√	optional	√	√
In-hand								
Broodmares	in-hand	n/a	n/a	√	√	n/a	√	√
Foals	in-hand	n/a	n/a	√	×	n/a	optional	foal slip
Youngstock	in-hand	n/a	n/a	√	unusual	n/a	√	mild bit if required

ABOVE *The true elegance of the hack is clearly seen in Keston Refund, shown so effectively by Miss S. Wyman. Quality, presence and lightness, accentuated by a neat, double bridle with a coloured browband, and diamonds and shark's teeth on the quarters, combine to make an excellent example of hack presentation.*

BELOW *Alison Tucker and Silver Spirit cantering during the judging of the hack championship at the Royal International Horse Show. The white girth has been used to advantage on this grey horse, and the pelham bridle with two reins is perfectly acceptable in this show class.*

Ladies' hacks making an attractive scene in front of the lake at Birmingham's Royal International Horse Show. They should be beautifully schooled and a lovely light, easy ride.

COBS

The cob is a small, chunky, weight-carrying horse. It must be beautifully mannered and a good comfortable easy ride – the sort of animal you would be happy to put your grandfather on. Cobs are judged like hunters and are expected to be good gallopers. Manners are essential and the whole outlook should be one of a calm but workmanlike performance. The cob should not exceed 15.1 hh and can be shown in lightweight or heavyweight classes as appropriate.

Working cobs are expected to jump at a good pace round a course of working-hunter-type jumps, and they must gallop.

In affiliated classes cobs must be registered, as must exhibitors and riders, with the British Show Hack, Cob and Riding Horse Association.

The cob should be a good, well-schooled ride, able to gallop and capable of carrying weight. Bill Bryan on the grand cob Barty.

COBS

	Show	Ridden by judge	Galloped	Plain browband	Tack	Martingale	Hogged mane	Plaited or pulled tail	Height certificate
Lightweight and heavyweight up to 15.1 hh	×	√	√	√	double bridle or pelham	×		√	√
Novice show	×	√	√	√	double bridle or pelham	×		√	√
Novice working	×	√	√	√	any	optional	√	√	√
Working	×	√	√	√	any	optional	√	√	√

Robert Oliver looks happy sitting on his champion cob. Although there are usually two weight classes – lightweight and heavyweight – the cob must not exceed 15.1 hh.

RIDING HORSES

The riding horse should have quality, substance, good bone, correct conformation, presence and true, straight action. It should be the sort of horse that falls between being a true hunter and true hack but sufficiently up to weight to carry an average adult. It should be a good well-trained ride and able to gallop. There is strong emphasis on ride and manners.

In affiliated classes exhibitors, riders and horses must be registered with the British Show Hack, Cob and Riding Horse Association. There are two classes: exceeding 14.2 hh but not exceeding 15.2 hh; and exceeding 15.2 hh. Height certificates will be required for horses entering the smaller height section.

RIDING HORSES

	Show	Ridden by judge	Galloped	Jumped	Height certificate	Mane plaited	Coloured browband	Double bridle or pelham
Small exc. 14.2 not exc. 15.2 *Large* exc. 15.2	√	√	√	occasionally in unaffiliated	√ / ×	√	optional	√
Novice	√	√	√	×	×	√	optional	√
Ladies	√	√	√	×	×	√	optional	√

Mrs R. Oliver on Bijoux, winner of the large riding horse class at the Royal International Horse Show. The riding horse has a little more substance than the hack but not quite as much as the hunter. It must be a lovely ride and well mannered.

SIDE-SADDLE CLASSES

The art of side-saddle riding is becoming increasingly popular once more and not only are there the Side-Saddle Association equitation classes but also working hunter, show-jumping, turn-out and dressage classes. There are still, of course, the more traditional classes for ladies' hacks, hunters, children's ponies, etc.

This ancient and extremely elegant form of riding is not particularly difficult to learn and most horses and ponies take to it readily if they are well schooled and going well on the flat. The side-saddle horse needs to have a good wither so that the saddle sits well and is a good fit.

The Side-Saddle Association is the governing body.

Juniors wear a hunting cap with habit and collar and tie for side-saddle classes. Dark gloves should be worn and hair neatly kept back. Any ribbons should be black or blue in colour.

SIDE-SADDLE CLASSES

	Set test	Show	Ridden by judge	Plaited	Galloped	Jumped	Veil	Bowler hat	Top hat – champs and evening
Equitation	√	n/a	n/a	√	×	×	√ adults	√	optional
Hacks and riding horses	×	√	√	√	rh √ h ×	×	√	√	√
Hunters	×	×	√	√	√	×	√	√	√
Ponies	×	√	×	√	rarely	×	×	×	×
Working hunter	n/a	×	optional	√	√	√	√	√	as necessary

Adults wear a bowler hat with veil, collar and tie. In the evening or at Royal shows for finals and championships it is correct to wear a top hat and veil with a hunting tie.

SHOW PONIES

Show ponies can be divided into three distinct types: the show pony, working hunter pony, and show hunter pony.

The show pony is the finest, possessing the most quality but maintaining the pony characteristics of being neat, not too wide and having an excellent temperament suitable for a child. Straight, smooth action and good general conformation with perfect manners are the essentials for all children's ponies.

The working hunter pony is a chunky, stronger type of pony, not requiring the quality of the show pony but possessing more substance. It is required to jump a course of rustic fences according to its height.

The show hunter pony is generally expected to fall inbetween the above two types, not necessarily having the substance of the working hunter pony nor the quality of the show pony. Nevertheless it should be of excellent conformation and with presence. It is not required to jump.

There is a wide variety of classes for ponies of all sizes suitable for children of different age groups, both at novice or open standard. There are also leading rein, first ridden, side-saddle, pair and team classes. Show hunter and working hunter ponies have height classes from 12 hh–13 hh, exceeding 13 hh–14 hh and exceeding 14 hh–

Mark Wilder on Little Diamond wins the show hunter pony class at the Royal International Horse Show. This exceptional pony has excelled in both show hunter and working hunter pony classes. The show hunter class has become very popular, with four different height sections. Show hunter ponies are not required to jump.

15 hh. Show ponies are up to 12.2 hh, exceeding 12.2 hh, not exceeding 13.2 hh, and exceeding 13.2 hh and not exceeding 14.2 hh. There are also height restrictions for leading rein at 11.2 hh, first ridden at 12 hh, and some 15 hh classes.

Pony breeding and youngstock classes are also very popular, catering for all sizes, stallions, broodmares, colts and fillies.

The British Show Pony Society is the governing body for all ridden show pony classes at affiliated shows. Height certificates are required.

Samantha Gilmore has Little Diamond beautifully balanced to win the working hunter pony championship. Working hunter ponies can be jumped in any tack but must keep this tack throughout the class. Riders must wear crash hats for the jumping phase.

Tony Hall on Cratfield Fairy Gold wins the show pony championship at the Highland Show. Pony and rider are correctly turned out for the class.

113

SHOW PONIES

	Show	Galloped in class	Galloped in show	Stripped	Jumped	Side-saddle	Shoeing	Spurs
Show ponies	√	according to class		√	×	optional	optional	×
Show hunter ponies	√	according to class		√	×	optional	optional	×
Working hunter ponies	√	√	√	if time permits	√	×	optional	×
Leading rein	led in-hand	×	×	√	×	×	optional	×
First ridden	√	×	×	√	×	×	optional	×
Side-saddle	√	judge's discretion	√	√	×	√	optional	×
Pairs	√	×	√	optional	×	optional	optional	×
Novices, show	√	according to class		√	×	optional	optional	×
Pony breeding classes	in-hand	n/a	n/a	n/a	n/a	n/a	optional	n/a

Show ponies continued

	Crash cap	Snaffle bridle	Whips not to exceed 30ins	4-year-olds and over	Height certificate	Age limit for rider	Plaited
Show ponies	×	any	√	3-y-o accepted in novice classes after 1st July	√	√	√
Show hunter ponies	×	any	√	3-y-o accepted in novice classes after 1st July	√	√	√
Working hunter ponies	√ in phase I	any	√	√	√	√	√
Leading rein	×	√	√	√	√	√	√
First ridden	×	√	√	√	√	√	√
Side-saddle	×	any	√	√	√	√	√
Pairs	×	any	√	√	√	√	√
Novices, show	×	√	√	√	√	√	√
Pony breeding classes	n/a	suitable bridle or headcollar	n/a	n/a	may be required for broodmares	n/a	√

Leading-rein classes are usually well filled! Ponies for this and the first ridden must be shown in snaffle bridles.

Pony youngstock classes usually come under the jurisdiction of the breed shows and cater for ponies of riding pony type, etc. likely to reach a certain height at maturity. They should be shown trimmed and plaited.

MOUNTAIN AND MOORLAND PONIES

Mountain and moorland ponies, the nine native breeds, are catered for in a wide variety of classes either as pure-breds, ridden or in-hand in breeds, or as mixed classes which are often split up to cater for the different heights, usually for those not exceeding 13 hh and for those exceeding 13 hh. The Welsh Cob Section D has no height limit but other breeds must conform to the height limits laid down by the various breed societies.

The native ponies are all named after the regions of Britain where they have bred and run wild for years. The nine breeds are Connemara, Dale, Dartmoor, Exmoor, Fell, Highland, New Forest, Shetland, and Welsh.

The smaller breeds are Dartmoor, Exmoor, Shetland, Welsh Mountain Section A and Welsh Pony Section B.

The larger breeds are Dales, Fell, Connemara, New Forest, High-

Mixed mountain and moorland classes cater for all nine of the British native breeds and sometimes allow other breeds to compete as well. Andrew Cousins on Cantref Glory, a Welsh Section A, beats the Connemara in this mountain and moorland championship.

land, Welsh Pony (Cob type) Section C and Welsh Cob Section D.

The classes for affiliated shows, other than specific breed classes, are working hunter pony, mountain and moorland driving classes and riding pony breed and ridden classes.

At some shows ponies other than the British native breeds are catered for in certain classes such as Haflingers, Norwegian Fjord, Icelandic, etc.

The National Pony Society governs the overall organisation of mountain and moorland ponies.

MOUNTAIN AND MOORLAND PONIES

	Measured or height certs (except Welsh see D)	Ridden by judge	Galloped	Coloured browbands (brass optional)	Rider age limit
In-hand	√	✕	✕	✕	✕
Youngstock	√	✕	✕	✕	✕
Working hunter pony	√	(unusual) ✕	√	✕	✕
Driving	√	✕	✕	✕	✕
Pony breeding	√	n/a	n/a	✕	n/a
Mixed M and M	√	√	√	✕	✕
Pure-bred	√	usually	√	✕	✕

Mountain and Moorland ponies continued

	Registration required for pure-breds	Whip length	Spurs	Plaited	Welsh sec A-D 1 single plait long behind ears	Dales mane and tail braiding
In-hand	√	n/a	✕	✕	optional	optional
Youngstock	√	n/a	✕	✕	optional	optional
Working hunter pony	√	30 ins	✕	✕	optional	optional
Driving	√	n/a	✕	✕	optional	optional
Pony breeding	√	n/a	✕	✕	optional	optional
Mixed M and M	√	30 ins	✕	✕	optional	optional
Pure-bred	√	30 ins	✕	✕	optional	optional

CONNEMARA

The Connemara pony originates from the west of Ireland in the area of Connaught. This particularly bleak and tough moorland has been home to the Connemara for several centuries. The height of the Connemara varies from 12–14.2 hh. The most dominant colour is grey but there are dun, brown, bay and black ponies, and the occasional roan or chestnut.

Connemaras are compact, deep, standing on short legs and covering a lot of ground. They have a well-balanced head and neck and free, easy, true movement. They have approximately 7–8 ins (17.5–20 cm) of bone below the knee. Their main characteristics are their hardiness of constitution, staying power, docility, intelligence and soundness. They are particularly versatile, excelling in children's competitions and in working hunter and show hunter pony classes.

The governing body for the Connemara pony is the English Connemara Pony Society.

The Connemara originated from the west of Ireland and is often dun or grey in colour. They are intelligent and versatile and have excelled in many different fields. They should be shown tidied but natural.

DALES

The Dales ponies are bred on the eastern hills of the Pennines. The Dales is closely related to the Fell pony, which is bred on the western side. Primarily bred as a pack pony, the Dales' main features are its strength, energy and intelligence.

The Dales pony should have a neat pony-like head, with ears that curve inwards slightly. The neck should be long and strong, the shoulders sloping and the withers fine. The hindquarters should be deep, lengthy and powerful, and the leg should have good bone measuring up to 9 ins (22.5 cm). The height of the Dales pony varies from 13.2–14.2 hh. The Dales is distinguished by great flexion of the joints which produces a high knee and hock action.

The Dales are used as all-round utility ponies capable of jumping and trekking. They are very popular for harness work.

The Dales Pony Society is the governing body for Dales.

Dales are strong ponies with high knee and hock action. They possess quite a lot of feather but usually have a neat pony-like head and stand between 13.2 hh and 14.2 hh.

DARTMOOR PONY

The Dartmoor pony breeds and runs wild on Dartmoor, Devon. It is known for its quiet, kind, reliable temperament. The maximum height is 12.2 hh and bay, brown, black and grey are the most common colours, with roans and chestnuts occasionally being found. Skewbalds and piebalds are not allowed.

The Dartmoor is a sturdy pony with particularly good conformation. It has a small, elegant head with small, alert ears. The neck is strong but not too heavy. The loins and hindquarters are strong and muscular. The limbs have a medium amount of bone. The pony moves with free, low strides that make it a particularly comfortable ride and an ideal child's first pony.

The Dartmoor Pony Society is the governing body.

The Dartmoor is a sturdy pony with excellent conformation and a small, elegant head. Many champion show ponies can claim a fair amount of Dartmoor in their breeding.

EXMOOR PONY

The Exmoor pony originates from Exmoor and is claimed to be the oldest of Britain's native ponies. The Exmoors that remained in the West Country have not been crossbred and are consequently a remarkably pure breed. The Exmoor rarely exceeds 12.3 hh and is bay, brown or dun with mealy marking on the muzzle round the eyes and inside the flanks. There are no visible white markings.

The Exmoor is typically 'pony' with particularly short thick ears. The neck is fairly long, the chest is deep and wide and the back is broad and level as far as the loins. The legs are short and well apart. The Exmoor has a very thick coat in the winter to help insulate it against the cold; the summer coat is hard and bright. The Exmoor moves well and quite low to the ground.

The Exmoor Pony Society is the governing body.

The Exmoor is one of the most ancient native breeds and is distinguished by its mealy eyes, nose and flank areas. They are sturdy and tough with a thick winter coat.

FELL PONY

The Fell pony is closely related to the Dales pony. It originates from the western side of the Pennine hills. Its height varies from 13.1–14 hh and it is usually black, brown or grey in colour, although a little amount of white is allowed.

The Fell is a tough, hardy, eye-catching pony with a great deal of strength. Fell ponies have a longish neck with a pony head. The quarters are muscular and strong, and the breed has good bone and strong limbs. Fells are renowned for their energetic action which is free and straight.

The Fell Pony Society, the governing body, was formed in 1912 and has helped to ensure the continuance of the breed. Fells are used for trekking, driving, and trail riding and as all-round utility ponies.

The Fell pony is similar to the Dales but has free, straight action and is renowned for its energy and strength. Many Fells are shown with traditional ribbon attached to their mane, as shown in this photograph.

HIGHLAND PONY

This pony breed originates from the Highlands in Scotland and has been part of the history there for centuries. Their height varies from 13–14.2 hh and the typical colours are various shades of dun, grey, brown or black, with the occasional bay and liver chestnut being seen. Most have a dorsal eel stripe running down the backbone and many have stripey markings inside the forelegs.

Highland ponies are particularly hardy and this enables them to live outside all year round. They are intelligent, strong, docile and sure-footed and one of the most versatile of the native ponies. Today many Highland ponies are shown under saddle and are frequently put to use carrying tourists across the steep terrain of the Scottish Highlands. They are still used as work ponies in Scottish forests and are employed in stag hunting. Highlands have a strong neck and a wide but fairly short head. The back is compact and deep and the quarters are power-ful. The legs are short, strong and with good-shaped hooves. There is a little silky feather on the legs and manes and tails are profuse.

The Highland Pony Society is the governing body.

Highlands are probably the most versatile of the native ponies, being particularly hardy, strong but docile. They have a little silky feather with profuse manes and tails. Many have a dorsal eel stripe and zebra marking on their legs.

123

NEW FOREST PONY

The New Forest pony originates from the New Forest in Hampshire where it runs wild and breeds. It is the second largest of the mountain and moorland breeds. Throughout the years many ponies of different breeds – Arabs, Thoroughbreds, etc. – have been let loose on the Forest to improve the breed. The New Forest is a mixture of the strength, agility and intelligence of the native British pony but is of a narrower frame. It is a very versatile pony. Its maximum height is 14 hh and few ponies are found to be under 12 hh. Bay and brown ponies are most usual but all colours are acceptable, except piebald, skewbald or blue-eyed cream. This riding type of pony has substance, with a pony-type head, sloping shoulder, a deep body, strong quarters, good bone and straight legs. The New Forest is ideal for children but can also be ridden by adults.

The New Forest Pony Breeding and Cattle Society is the governing body.

The New Forest is of a narrower frame than most native ponies and with no feather. It is popular as a children's riding pony, being very versatile. This pony shows off its paces well in front of the judge.

SHETLAND PONY

This pony originates from the Shetland Islands. It is the smallest British mountain and moorland pony, measuring not more than 10.2 hh. The ponies may be bay, brown, chestnut, grey or part-colours but black is the foundation colour. The Shetland is incredibly strong relative to its size, therefore it excels in harness work; as a pack pony it is able to carry more weight in proportion to its size than any other pony or horse in the world.

The Shetland's head has a broad forehead with a straight face. The neck is slightly crested and of a good length. The shoulder is sloping and the body deep. The Shetland pony grows two layers of coat in the winter, which is a particularly unusual feature.

The Shetland was the first British native pony to have its own breed society, which was started in 1890. The Shetland Pony Stud Book Society is the governing body.

The smallest of the British native breeds, the Shetland is the strongest pony for its size in the world. They make good children's lead-rein ponies and are extremely tough, having two layers of coat in the winter.

WELSH PONIES

The Welsh ponies are perhaps Britain's most beautiful native pony. Coming from the Welsh hills they are strong and tough but renowned for their exquisite heads and floating action. They have good temperaments but also have plenty of dash and jumping ability and make excellent children's ponies for all ages and sizes.

The stud book has been divided into four sections to cater for the different heights and type of pony. These are:

Section A   Welsh Mountain Ponies (not exceeding 12 hh)
Section B   Welsh Ponies (not exceeding 13.2 hh)
Section C   Welsh Ponies – cob type (not exceeding 13.2 hh)
Section D   Welsh Cobs

A recent innovation has been the introduction of a new section (E) for geldings.

In mountain and moorland qualifiers and working hunter pony classes, Section Ds have to be 14.2 hh or under.

The Welsh Pony and Cob Society is the governing body for all Welsh ponies.

The Welsh are divided into groups according to their size and type. This beautiful Section A is the smallest type. Section As should not exceed 12 hh and are known as Welsh mountain ponies.

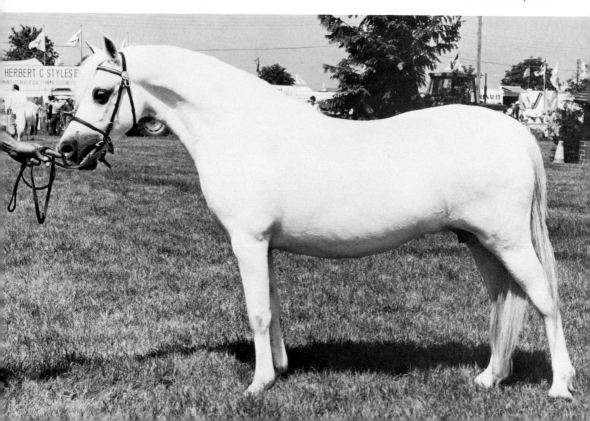

The Welsh Section B does not exceed 13.2 hh. This pony has the traditional single long plait put in just behind the ears.

Welsh Section C ponies are of cob type; they should not exceed 13.2 hh. This dramatic picture shows them parading at the trot. Be sure your handler can run and has suitable shoes!

The Welsh cob, Section D, exceeds 13.2 hh and is a fine strong type. In mountain and moorland qualifiers and for working hunter pony classes, Section D's may not exceed 14.2 hh.

ARABS

The Arab is an ancient breed with a distinctive appearance, and as with all breeds its type and conformation are important.

The head should be small and wedge shaped, broad at the cheek bones and relatively short. The forehead should be wide between the eyes and fairly flat. The eyes should be large and shaped like a blunted oval with wide, finely edged nostrils. Ears should be small, set wide apart and quick and alert. The neck should be long and well curved and is carried rather higher and more proudly than in most breeds.

The chest should be wide and deep, with the loins short and strong. The back is short and level. The body is well rounded and the quarters long from the hip to the point of buttocks.

The tail carriage is one of the most distinguishing features of the breed. It should be set level with the back and carried high. Manes and tails should be free, flowing and silky.

There are classes for pure-breds, part-breds and Anglo-Arabs, both ridden and in-hand. Ridden Arabs are treated as any other riding horse. There are sometimes novice as well as side-saddle classes and in-hand classes cater for stallions, broodmares and youngstock.

At affiliated shows horses, riders and owners must be registered with and members of the Arab Horse Society.

The pure-bred Arab has perhaps one of the most dramatic profiles, with its distinctive head and tail carriage. Shown with mane and tail flowing naturally, they make a fine sight at the Royal International Horse Show.

ARABS

Ridden	Show	Galloped	Mane plaited	Tail plaited	Tack	Stripped	Ridden by judge
Pure-bred	√ usually	usually	×	×	suitable for class	√	√
Anglo- and part-bred	√ usually	usually	√	√	as above	√	√
Side-saddle	√ usually	optional	not pure-breds		as above	√	√
Novice	√ usually	optional	not pure-breds		as above	√	√
In-hand							
Pure-bred	√	n/a	×	×	show bridle or strong Arab-style bridle	n/a	n/a
Part-bred	√	n/a	√	√	show bridle	n/a	n/a
Stallions and colts	√	n/a	not pure-breds		adequately bitted	n/a	n/a
Mares	√	n/a	not pure-breds		show bridle	n/a	n/a
Youngstock	√	n/a	not pure-breds		show bridle	n/a	n/a

There are many classes for Anglo- and part-bred Arabs, the former being crossed with the Thoroughbred and the latter having some Arab in its breeding. This two-year-old Anglo-Arab shows many of the Arab features in its head.

129

HACKNEYS

Originally a saddle horse, the Hackney was developed from trotting horses around East Anglia and Yorkshire during the eighteenth and nineteenth centuries. Hackneys are renowned for their distinctive high-stepping action and are now almost exclusively used for driving, for which sport they have become extremely popular worldwide.

The Hackney horse may be any height from 14.1 hh (approx.) to well over 16 hh, while the Hackney pony is any height up to 14 hh and is virtually a breed of its own.

The shoulder and knee action is free and high and the foreleg is thrown well forward with a slight pause to give the unique Hackney movement. This is partly inherited and partly taught through the use of heavy shoes and special training. The hind action is also exaggerated.

Usually bay, dark brown or black with the occasional chestnut, Hackneys are compact, with short legs and strong hocks, and a fine but small head carried high on an arched neck.

HACKNEYS	Height certificates	Trot or jog	Cantering	Top rein	Stand up cruppers	Plaited and knotted with cord	Tails plaited or pulled	Nicking or docking
In-hand								
1, 2, 3 year olds	√	√	×	optional	optional	√	×	×
4 years and over	√	√	×	optional	optional	√	×	×
Mares	√	√	×	×	×	√	×	×
Stallions	√	√	×	optional	optional	√	×	×
Driven								
Amateur	n/a	√	×	optional	√	√	×	×
Open	n/a	√	×	optional	√	√	×	×
Single	n/a	√	×	optional	√	√	×	×
Pair	n/a	√	×	optional	√	√	×	×
Team	n/a	√	×	optional	√	√	×	×
Ordinary driving	n/a	√	×	optional	√	√	×	×

Apart from appearing in specialist Hackney classes, they are used for all types of driving, including combined driving and marathons.

The Hackney Horse Society is the governing body.

One of the greatest Hackney producers in the world, Mrs Frank Haydon, trains her horses and ponies to move to perfection.

WARMBLOODS

There are several different strains of warmblood horse which have evolved from crossing the Thoroughbred with the cold-blooded breeds of Europe to produce a more useful performance horse suitable for today's highly competitive activities.

Each different breed that has been used has its own particular attributes and when crossed with the Thoroughbred has produced a particularly successful 'marriage'. A tractable temperament is one of the main characteristics which has made these horses so successful for dressage, show jumping and driving. Warmblood breeding has been well established on the Continent for some time but the setting up of the British Warmblood Society has been a recent innovation over here.

A fine example of a British warmblood, Catherston Dutch Bid has proved himself a first-class performance horse in many spheres. Primarily a top dressage horse, he is seen here taking part in a working hunter class at the Royal Show, with Jennie Loriston-Clarke on board.

There are strict grading rules for registration papers for all warmbloods and they are shown in-hand, under saddle and judged on performance.

The main governing bodies at present catering for Warmbloods are the British Warmblood Society, the British Trakehner Association and the Hanoverian Society.

WARMBLOODS

	In-hand (Continental)	Height certificates or measured	Registration papers	Coloured browband	Double bridles or pelhams	Plaited
Broodmares	√	√	√	✕	✕	√
Colts and fillies	√	✕	✕	✕	✕	optional
Youngstock	√	n/a	✕	✕	✕	optional
British sports horse	√	n/a	✕	✕	✕	√
Mare grading	√	n/a	n/a	✕	✕	√
Stallion progeny	√	n/a	n/a	✕	✕	optional

PALOMINOS

The term 'palomino' refers to a colour and not to a breed. Palominos, therefore, may be found amongst many types of horse and pony with colour being the main priority.

There are in-hand classes for all age groups as well as a ridden class, and these are judged in the usual way. The judge may ride exhibits and ask to see them galloped.

Palominos must not be plaited as the colour of their manes and tails is taken into serious consideration. There should not be more than twenty-five per cent dark hairs and the coat should be the colour of a newly minted gold coin. Coats that are too dark or a wishy washy colour will be penalised.

The British Palomino Society is the governing body.

PALOMINOS

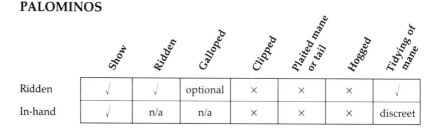

	Show	Ridden	Galloped	Clipped	Plaited mane or tail	Hogged	Tidying of mane
Ridden	√	√	optional	×	×	×	√
In-hand	√	n/a	n/a	×	×	×	discreet

The palomino should be shown in its natural state, with free-flowing mane and tail, and unclipped. There are several in-hand classes as well as ridden ones.

134

BRITISH SPOTTED PONIES

This fairly rare but popular pony has existed in Britain for centuries. Although there are few rules for judging, good basic conformation is vitally important and two different types exist: (a) riding type; and (b) driving type, including cobs. They may be of any size up to and including 14.2 hh.

Colouring may be leopard, snowflake or blanket. Some young animals in particular have a pronounced roan colour which does not debar them but a more boldly marked colour is preferred. Typical characteristics are white sclera round the eye, hooves yellowish white with vertical stripes and mottled flesh marks on the bare skin. Most ponies are shown in their natural state and are usually ridden by the judge. Coloured browbands are best avoided as they detract from the colouring of the animal.

The British Spotted Pony Society maintains a register for stallions, mares and geldings of known breeding. At present there is a temporary entry scheme for ponies of unknown or unregistered breeding which conform to the required breed characteristics.

BRITISH SPOTTED PONIES

	Show	Ridden by judge	Plaited	Plain browband	Stripped	Galloped
Ridden	√	×	×	√	√	√
In-hand	n/a	n/a	×	√	n/a	n/a

British spotted pony. This ancient but spectacular pony has existed in Britain for centuries. It should have good basic conformation and the colouring may be leopard, snowflake or blanket. Shown in their natural state they are best produced in plain tack.

135

APPALOOSAS

The distinctive Appaloosa has spread from America and now boasts the third largest number of breed registrations in the world. The spotted appearance of the coat must also include a mottled skin and a white sclera round the eye. They often possess thin, wispy manes and tails, and have striped feet. There are five main coat patterns: leopard spotted, blanket spotted, snowflake, frost and marble.

This American breed now boasts the third largest breed registrations in the world. Shown in plain tack, in-hand or ridden, the Appaloosa is versatile and has five main coat patterns: leopard (shown), blanket, spotted, snowflake and marble.

Appaloosas are used for numerous purposes – being strong, agile and hardy. In Britain and Europe they tend to be more of a hunter type, while in America and Australia they are more like a Quarter horse in type.

They are shown in-hand as well as ridden as general riding horses in Britain. Because of their sparse manes they may be shown hogged or as best suits the horse.

The British Appaloosa Society is the governing body.

APPALOOSAS

	Stripped	Ridden by judge	Galloped	Show	Coloured browband	Plaited	Side reins or rollers
In-hand	√	n/a	n/a	√	×	×	×
Stallions	√	√	√	√	×	×	×
Ridden	√	√	√	√	×	×	n/a
Working hunter	√	√	√	√	×	×	n/a

137

ANDALUSIANS, LUSITANOS AND LIPIZZANERS

THE ANDALUSIAN

The Andalusian hails from the Andalusian region of Spain and is shown mainly in its own breed classes. There are in-hand and ridden classes and the horses are shown with their long manes free flowing. There are two ridden classes: one is conducted in the standard way with competitors in conventional English dress and judged as a riding horse class. The other, a freestyle performance class, is ridden in Spanish dress and tack as used during fiestas. The riders give a three-minute freestyle display, which is judged fifty per cent on technical merit and fifty per cent on artistic impression.

Andalusians are fairly high-stepping horses but must also have reach. Dishing is not a fault in the breed neither are slight cow-hocks, although this should not be excessive.

The British Andalusian Horse Society is the governing body concerned with the Spanish horse in Great Britain.

Andalusians have their own breed classes and are shown in their natural state, with manes free-flowing. They may be shown ridden as a riding horse or in a freestyle performance class with Spanish dress and tack as seen in Spanish fiestas.

ANDALUSIANS, LUSITANOS AND LIPIZZANERS

	Ridden	Show	Ridden by judge	Plaited	Dress	Tack	Coloured browband	Height certificates
Ridden	√	√	optional	×	English	any	×	×
In-hand	×	√	n/a	×	n/a	show	×	×
Side-saddle	√	√	optional	×	traditional or English	double	×	×
Performance shows	√	√	optional	×	traditional or English	traditional or English	×	×
Driven	×	√	n/a	×	n/a	any	×	×

Plaited column note: occasionally running plait

THE LUSITANO

The Lusitano from Portugal is a relative of the Lipizzaner both being founded from Andalusian stock. A small, strong athletic horse with high, rounded movement, it has a wonderful temperament and was very popular with *rejoneadors* (bull-fighters) and for high-school movements. It is usually grey but may be any other solid colour and stands around 15–16 hh.

The Lusitano Breed Society is the governing body.

THE LIPIZZANER

This famous breed, so well known for its displays at the Spanish Riding School and worldwide, was originally started by Archduke Charles of Austria from imported Andalusian stock, and the original stud at Lipizza was set up. Usually grey in colour they may also be bay and are often born dark but lighten as they grow older. Extremely athletic, strong and intelligent with an excellent temperament, they excel at dressage and high-school work as well as carriage driving.

The Lipizzaner Society of Great Britain is the governing body.

Apart from pure-bred classes, Lipizzaners, Lusitanos and Andalusians are often shown together in ridden classes.

140

HAFLINGERS

This versatile, all-round, small horse is a native of the Austrian Alps and over the years has become popular in Britain both for riding and driving. Originally the breed was very sturdy and thick-set but nowadays a taller, finer horse is preferred.

Characteristics of the breed include the chestnut colouring and flaxen mane and tail, which is strictly adhered to. White stars, blazes or stripes are acceptable, but white on the limbs or body is discouraged.

The head should be small with a slight dish and large, dark, kindly eyes. The neck should be strong and well positioned but not short; the body should be broad and deep with a strong back and well-carried tail. Limbs should be clean and hard with healthy hooves. Strong forearms and a good second thigh with short cannons are favoured. Mares usually have between 6¾–7¾ ins (17–19.6 cm) of bone; stallions have 7¼–9 ins (18.4–22.8 cm). Haflingers are generally 13.1–14.2½ hh with very placid temperaments.

There are classes for in-hand, ridden and driven Haflingers. The animals are shown in their natural state, as for native breeds.

The Haflinger Society of Great Britain is the governing body and all competitors should be members and their horses currently registered.

HAFLINGERS

	Show	Ridden by judge	Tack	Stripped	Plaited
Ridden	√	√	any	√	✗
In-hand	√	n/a	plain	n/a	✗
Driven	√	n/a	—	n/a	✗

OPPOSITE ABOVE Lipizzaners, the breed associated with the Spanish Riding School, are shown in-hand and under saddle and are extremely athletic, with excellent temperaments. This stallion is typical of the breed, showing a high-crested neck with proud, noble bearing.

OPPOSITE BELOW A Haflinger. This tough little Austrian horse is easily recognisable by its chestnut colour and pale flaxen mane and tail. Popular for riding and driving it has its own breed show and performs in-hand, ridden and driven.

HEAVY HORSES

The heavy horses are undoubtedly amongst the most spectacular animals to be seen in the show ring.

The Shire, Clydesdale, Suffolk Punch and English Percheron are regularly shown throughout the country with a few Ardennes now appearing to join them.

The in-hand classes generally include those for mares (barren and in-foal), foals, yearlings, two- and three-year-olds, geldings, and occasionally stallions.

Harness classes include single and pairs with trade and agricultural

HEAVY HORSES

In-hand	White rope halter	Braided manes and tails	Half rig plait	Full rig plait
Youngstock	√ bit if required	√ tails only for foals	√ but not foals	√ but not foals
Mares – barren and in foal	√ —	√	√ Shires and Clydesdales	Percheron and Suffolk
Geldings	√	√	√ Shires and Clydesdales	Percheron and Suffolk
Stallions	× bridle with bit and harness	√	Shires and Clydesdales	Percheron and Suffolk
Driven				
Trade	n/a	√	Suffolk and Clydesdale	Percheron and Suffolk
Agricultural	n/a	√	Suffolk and Clydesdale	Percheron and Suffolk
Farmers' turn-out	n/a	√	Suffolk and Clydesdale	Percheron and Suffolk
Teams	n/a	√	Suffolk and Clydesdale	Percheron and Suffolk

vehicles, and sometimes farmers' turn-out classes. There are also classes for teams of threes and fours.

Each breed has a slightly different method of presentation – the Suffolk, for example, has a full rig plait just under the crown of the mane intertwined with bass or wool and topped with coloured wool pom-poms.

Shires are plaited with wool, bass or braid in a half-rig plait into which 'flights' are incorporated (these should be of an odd number). The Shire's knot on the tail is made with three separate strands of hair plaited under so that the 'bun' on top looks neat. A 'jug handle' or Yorkshire bob is often included, with two coloured ribbons added.

The Clydesdale usually has a tiny half rig plait along the top of the mane, which is braided. The flights, put in afterwards, should number eleven for in-hand classes and seven for harness.

Percherons, like the Suffolks, have a full rig plait but on top of the neck and are fully braided with knotted tails.

The colours most frequently used for braiding are red, yellow, blue, green, orange and white; and only two colours should ever be used together.

The tails of foals are often braided but their manes are always left loose.

Heavy horse turnout is something that must be learned from an expert. Tails can be put up as a knot in the form of a bun, with either a jug handle (as shown) or Yorkshire bob with ribbons added.

143

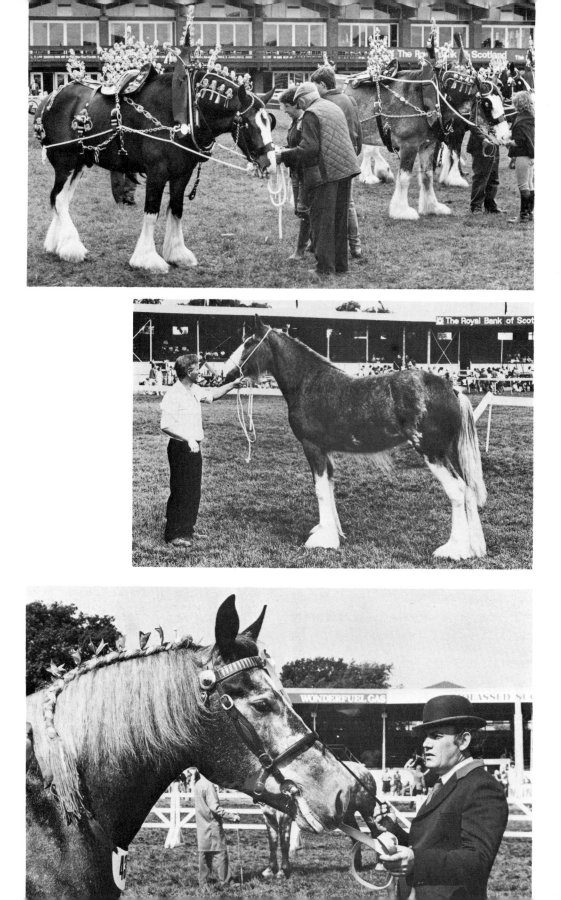

CLYDESDALE

The Clydesdale originates from Scotland where it has worked for many years on the farms and in the forests. Its colours are bay, brown, roan and occasionally black. A white stripe on the face, white markings on the underside of the body, and white stockings up to and over the knees and hocks are common. Its height ranges from 16.3 hh to 18 hh and it is immensely strong; it is one of the world's most popular work horses. A distinguishing feature of the Clydesdale is the abundance of fine, silky feather on the legs. The Clydesdale moves with enormous energy, spring and power.

Today the Clydesdale is shown in heavy turn-out classes and in-hand.

The Clydesdale was the first of the British heavy horses to have its own society, starting in 1877. This has ensured good breeding throughout the years.

PERCHERON

The Percheron is a type of heavy draught horse originating from France from an area called La Perche. It is a particularly good-looking heavy horse and has enormous muscular development. It has ample bone and gives an impression of good balance and power. The Percheron varies in height from 16 hh to at least 17.1 hh, and is either grey or black in colour. It moves very well for its size and despite its good temperament is not at all sluggish. With a fairly high influence of Arab in its original breeding there is a trace of elegance in this heavy horse.

Percherons are still used today for agricultural work and are shown and driven all over the world. One of the unusual features of the Percheron horse is that it has a *very* small amount of feather on the legs.

The British Percheron Society was formed in 1918 and is still the governing body for the breed.

OPPOSITE ABOVE *Presentation at its best. Few sights can be more impressive or require greater preparation than the heavy-horse decorated harness classes.*

OPPOSITE CENTRE *A fine young Clydesdale showing the markings and colouring typical of the breed. Youngstock do not have their manes plaited but may have their tails braided*

OPPOSITE *The distinctive head and coat of the Percheron, which is usually grey or black in colour.*

145

SHIRE HORSE

The Shire horse originates from the Midlands and Fens in Britain and is the tallest and heaviest breed amongst the cold-bloods. Stallions and geldings are often as high as 18 hh. Black is the most common colour for Shires, with bays, browns and greys being seen less often. Most showing Shires have a large amount of white on their legs up to the knee and hock joint.

This huge horse has a remarkably docile temperament, which could perhaps be due to its quick maturity – it is often worked at three years old. In the past the Shire was used in industry, agriculture and transportation. Nowadays it is a popular show horse and draught worker for displays and brewery firms.

Shires have a long lean head with a slight Roman nose. The eyes are very docile in expression and the neck long and slightly arched. They have short legs with short cannons and a good amount of bone, up to 11 ins (27.5 cm). They have powerful and straight movement. A particular characteristic is the copious amount of silky feather on the legs.

The Shire Horse Society is the governing body.

A wonderful stamp of Shire horse shown in a halter with bit attached, and showing the wool plaited along the mane in a half rig plait into which an odd number of 'flights' have been incorporated.

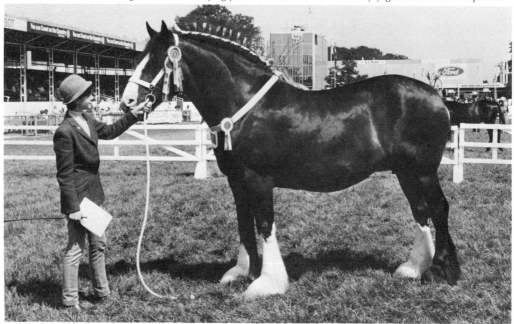

SUFFOLK PUNCH

The Suffolk Punch originates from Suffolk and is the smallest of the heavy horses, measuring between 16 hh and 17 hh. It is always chestnut with no markings except occasionally a small white star on the face. The seven chestnut colours vary in shade from light to dark but by far the most common is bright chestnut. The Suffolk Punch is thought to be the original war-horse and is the purest British cold-blood breed. It has great width and is tremendously deep; it is enormously powerful and very well put together. It is considered most suitable for agricultural work, having very little feather.

The Suffolk Breed Society was formed in 1877 and is still the governing body for the breed.

The chestnut colouring of the Suffolk Punch is a distinctive hall-mark of this heavy horse breed. Shown in-hand and driven it is thought to be the original war-horse. As can be seen, it is a powerfully built animal.

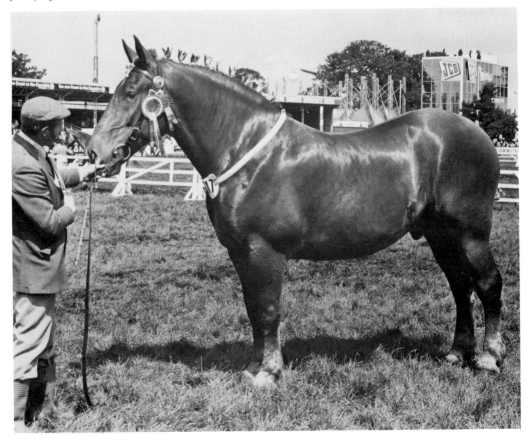

IRISH DRAUGHT

The Irish Draught was originally a farm horse in Ireland but its history is somewhat obscure. Usually it varies between 15 hh and 17 hh and is bay, brown, grey or chestnut with a small intelligent head. The body should be deep with a good shoulder, clean limbs with flat bone and strong but not overlarge feet. There should be no feather.

A stud book was started in Ireland in 1917 and in 1976 the Irish Draught Horse Society was formed to promote and preserve the breed. In 1979 the British Irish Horse Society was formed which has introduced a strict inspection scheme for stallions and mares as well as a registration system. The Irish Draught has produced excellent competition horses when crossed with the Thoroughbred.

Irish Draughts are shown only in-hand. They are highly sought after by breeders – when crossed with the Thoroughbred they produce good competition horses.

CLEVELAND BAYS

The Cleveland Bay is one of the oldest British breeds. Originally used as pack horses they have since become outstanding carriage horses. They are often crossed with Thoroughbreds to produce top competition horses for all disciplines, and hunters with substance and quality.

Clevelands are very strong with characteristics to match. They are always bay in colour with black points. They possess good jumping ability and free, straight action. They should have a bold head carried on a long neck, and strong well-shaped feet – blue in colour. Shallow or narrow feet are undesirable. Clevelands are usually about 16–16.2 hh and are shown only in-hand in their pure-bred form.

The Cleveland Bay Horse Society is the governing body.

This tough breed, always bay in colour, is shown only in-hand in pure-bred classes. They have produced excellent competition horses when crossed with the Thoroughbred and have made outstanding driving horses.

AMERICAN HORSES

The American horse has become increasingly popular in Britain and the three main breeds – the Morgan Horse, the Quarter Horse and Saddlebred – have their own set of rules for in-hand and ridden classes, though the latter have been somewhat modified to suit British standards.

Western riding is now very popular and classes catering for Western pleasure horses, Western horsemanship, Western riding pattern, trail horses, stock horses, reining patterns, versatility (Western and English) and cattle roping.

There are three Western rule books used in the UK and although each has slight variations the principles are similar.

Western riding classes have become extremely popular with many of the best horses coming from the versatile Quarter horse. These riders show off Western dress. Notice the typical slit-ear bridle, so popular out West, which is quick and easy to put on.

In-hand classes are open to all breeds as it is the handler being judged rather than the horse, but horses must be in show condition (it is the rider who is being judged in the Western horsemanship classes also).

The governing bodies for American horses and Western Riding include: the British Morgan Horse Society, the British Quarter Horse Association, the American Saddlebred Association of Great Britain, the Western Horseman's Association of Great Britain, American Quarter Horse Association, and the Western Equestrian Society.

AMERICAN SADDLEBRED

The American Saddlebred, known as the all-American Horse, is a versatile breed but perhaps best known in Britain as a show horse. At present it performs only in walk, trot and canter, but in America it demonstrates two further acquired gaits, the rack and the slow gait, unique to the breed. The horse should give the illusion of being about to explode whilst remaining mannerly. The head should be held extremely high and ridden in the American saddle-seat style. The action should contain plenty of knee action but cover the ground lightly and rapidly. When standing the American Saddlebred should 'park' in the style of a Hackney. The classes are divided into Western as per Western Horsemen Association Rules or English as required per class. Spurs are permissible but not with snaffle bridles.

Further information can be obtained from the American Saddlebred Association of Great Britain.

QUARTER HORSE

The Quarter horse possesses tremendous power in its hindquarters, with its hocks placed well underneath it, and is considered the fastest horse over a ¼-mile sprint. It is extremely agile, with a wonderful temperament and its versatility has resulted in its being the most numerous breed in the USA. It usually stands between 14.3 hh and 16 hh.

The British Quarter Horse Association Ltd is the governing body.

MORGAN HORSE

This is the oldest of America's light breeds. It originated from one small bay colt called Figure who was renamed Justin Morgan after his schoolteacher owner. Tough, agile, hardy and extremely fast, his progeny carried his strong characteristics which have changed remarkably little over the last two centuries. The breed has good conformation, being compact, well-muscled and stylish in appearance. Its high, proud head carriage gives the impression of the neck sitting on top of the withers. Being extremely versatile, Morgans are shown in-hand as well as driven and ridden.

The governing body for Morgans is the British Morgan Horse Society.

The Morgan's features can be clearly seen with its mane cut at the poll and distinctive American show bridle and bit. Morgans are shown in-hand, driven and ridden and are trained to stand in this traditional pose.

POLO PONIES

The polo pony has evolved from various athletic breeds; the type probably originated in Manipur, India, but as the sport spread to different countries each found its own ideal by crossbreeding, usually Thoroughbreds with local breeds. Nowadays the Argentinian polo pony is the most sought-after. Always called 'ponies' because they were approximately 14.3–15 hh, the modern polo pony now often reaches 15.3 hh.

Usually rather long and angular, particularly fast and quick, tough and agile, the polo pony is shown hogged with its tail knotted or braided up, booted or bandaged and ready to show its paces. There is no set pattern as there is no governing body for these horses. Shows that put on classes usually stipulate their own requirements.

CASPIAN HORSES

Normally between 10–12.2 hh the Caspian gives the appearance of a well-bred elegant horse in miniature. It has a fine, silky coat with the mane and tail of a Thoroughbred but the winter coat of a mountain pony. Caspians have a calm, alert and willing temperament and are extremely intelligent. They are extremely strong, jump well and are highly suitable as riding, driving and jumping ponies.

The British Caspian Society deals with all registrations, memberships, etc.

ICELANDIC HORSES

Icelandic horses, which not surprisingly originate from Iceland, vary in height from 12–14 hh. Most colours are found but the most common are dun and chestnut, including liver chestnut, with a flaxen mane and tail. They are very tough little ponies and many are exported; large numbers have been used as pit ponies in Britain. The Icelandic horse makes an ideal family mount and has great ability for trail riding.

Icelandic horses are shown but they are ridden in classes designed only to show the purity and quality of the gaits. The classes may include the four-gait class, which shows walk, trot, canter and *tolt* (a four-beat running walk). Sometimes there are pace tests where horses can sometimes reach up to 30 miles an hour. The Icelandic is not judged on looks but on ability as a riding horse and on its temperament and character.

The Icelandic is a stocky pony with a large head, intelligent eyes, and a short muscular neck with a thick mane. The body is compact, the quarters sloping and the limbs short and strong.

The Icelandic Horse Society is the governing body.

FJORD HORSES

The Fjord horse originates from Norway, although now it is found extensively in Scandinavia. Its height varies from 13.2–14.2 hh and its only coat colour is sandy. Its distinctive feature is its mane, which is blonde on the outside and has a black stripe running up the inside. The mane is trimmed with the blonde part being cut 1 in. (2.5 cm) shorter than the black part.

The Fjord horse has a long history as a work-horse, being used centuries ago by the Vikings; today it is still used for logging in Norway and all over Scandinavia. It is now bred for riding and driving and a lot of horses compete in dressage competitions. Fjords are often accepted into mountain and moorland classes although some smaller shows exclude them since they are not British mountain and moorland. They are shown trimmed and not plaited.

The Fjord Horse Society is the governing body.

THE FALABELLA

A 'new' breed which is appearing in the UK is the Falabella, one of the world's smallest breeds standing less than 8.2 hh. These have the appearance of scaled-down horses and are generally kept as pets. They are occasionally driven. They originate from Argentina.

The governing body is the Falabella Society.

The Falabella is the smallest breed in the world, standing less than 8.2 hh.

USEFUL ADDRESSES

American Saddlebred Association of Great Britain
Uplands
North Road
Alfriston
East Sussex
Tel: 0323 870295

Arab Horse Society
Goddards Green
Cranbrook
Kent TN17 3LP
Tel: 0580 713389

British Andalusian Horse Society
Church Farm
Church Street
Semington
Trowbridge
Wiltshire
Tel: 0380 870139

British Appaloosa Society
2 Fredrick Street
Rugby
Warwicks
Tel: 0788 860535

British Driving Society
27 Dugard Place
Barford
Nr Warwick CV35 8DX
Tel: 0926 624420

British Horse Society
British Equestrian Centre
Stoneleigh
Kenilworth
Warwickshire CV8 2LR
Tel: 0203 696697

British Lipizzaner Horse Society
Glynarthen
Llandysul
Dyfed SA44 6PB
Tel: 0239 810433

British Morgan Horse Society
George and Dragon Hall
Mary Place
London W11
Tel: 01-229 8155

British Palomino Society
Penrhiwllan
Llandysul
Dyfed SA44 5NZ
Tel: 023 975 387

British Percheron Horse Society
52A Broad Street
Ely
Cambs CB7 4AH
Tel: 0353 67005

British Quarter Horse Association Ltd
4th Street
NAC
Stoneleigh
Kenilworth
Warwickshire CV8 2LG
Tel: 0203 26850

British Show Hack, Cob, and Riding Horse
  Association
c/o Rookwood, Packington Park
Meriden
Warks CV7 7HF
Tel: 0676 23535

British Show Pony Society
124 Green End Road
Sawtry
Huntingdon
Cambs
Tel: 0487 831376

British Spotted Pony Society
c/o 17 School Lane
Dronfield
Sheffield
Yorkshire S18 6RY
Tel: 0246 413201

British Trakehner Association
Hallagenna Stud
St Breward
Cornwall
Tel: 0208 850439

British Warmblood Society
Moorlands Farm
New Yatt
Witney
Oxfordshire
Tel: 0993 86673

Caspian Pony Stud (UK) and Society
Hopstone Lea
Claverley
Salop
Tel: 07466 206

Cleveland Bay Horse Society
York Livestock Centre
Murton
York YO1 3UF
Tel: 0904 489731

Clydesdale Horse Society of Great Britain and
    Ireland
24 Beresford Terrace
Ayr
Ayrshire
Scotland
Tel: 0292 281650

Dales Pony Society
196 Springvale Road
Walkley
Sheffield
Yorks S6 3NU
Tel: 0742 683992

Dartmoor Pony Society
Fordons
17 Clare Court
New Biggin Street
Thaxted
Essex
Tel: 0371 830718

English Connemara Pony Society
2 The Leys, Salford
Chipping Norton
Oxon OX7 5FD
Tel: 0608 3309

Exmoor Pony Society
Glen Fern
Waddicombe
Dulverton
Somerset TA22 9RY
Tel: 03984 490

Falabella Society
c/o Kilverstone Wildlife Park
Thetford
Norfolk
Tel: 0842 5369

Fell Pony Society
19 Dragley Beck
Ulverston
Cumbria LA12 0HD
Tel: 0229 52742

Fjord Horse Society of Great Britain
Glynarthen
Llandysul
Dyfed SA44 6PB
Tel: 0239 810433

Hackney Horse Society
Clump Cottage
Chitterne
Warminster
Wiltshire
Tel: 0985 50906

Haflinger Society of Great Britain
13 Park Field
Pucklechurch
Bristol BS17 3NR
Tel: 027582 3479

Hanoverian Society
c/o British Warmblood Society
Moorlands Farm, New Yatt
Witney
Oxford
Tel: 0993 86673

Highland Pony Society
Orwell House
Milnathort
Kinross-shire KY13 7YQ
Tel: 0577 63495

Icelandic Horse Society of Great Britain
Rosebank, Higher Merley Lane
Corfe Mallen
Dorset BH21 3EG
Tel: 0202 886187

Irish Draught Horse Society of Great Britain
4th Street
NAC
Stoneleigh
Kenilworth
Warwickshire
Tel: 0203 26850

Ladies Side-Saddle Association
Highbury House
Welford
Northampton
Tel: 0858 81300

Lipizzaner Society of Great Britain
Starrock Stud
Ludwell
Wiltshire SP7 0PW
Tel: 0747 88639

Lusitano Breed Society
Fox Croft
Bulstrode Lane
Felden
Hemel Hempstead
Herts HP3 0PB
Tel: 0442 50806

National Light Horse Breeding Society (HIS)
96 High Street
Edenbridge,
Kent
Tel: 0732 866277

National Pony Society
Brook House, 25 High Street
Alton
Hants GU34 1AW
Tel: 0420 88333

New Forest Pony Breeding and Cattle Society
Beacon Cottage, Burley
Ringwood
Hants BH24 4EW
Tel: 04253 2272

Shetland Pony Stud-Book Society
Pedigree House
6 Kings Place
Perth
Scotland
Tel: 0738 23471

Shire Horse Society
East of England Showground
Peterborough PE2 0XE
Tel: 0733 234451

Suffolk Horse Society
6 Church Street
Woodbridge
Suffolk IP12 1DH
Tel: 0728 746534

Thoroughbred Breeders' Association
Stanstead House, The Avenue
Newmarket
Suffolk CB8 9AA
Tel: 0638 661321

Welsh Pony and Cob Society
6 Chalybeate Street
Aberystwyth
Dyfed SY23 1HS
Tel: 0970 617501

Western Horseman's Association of Great Britain
36 Old Fold View
Barnet
Herts

INDEX

Figures in *italics* refer to illustrations